NO ONE'S PERFECT

NO ONE'S PERFECT

Hirotada Ototake

Translated by Gerry Harcourt

KODANSHA INTERNATIONAL
Tokyo • New York • London

Acknowledgments

The author would like to express his heartfelt thanks to Ichiro Ozawa of Kodansha for all that he has done to bring this book to publication.

The translator wishes to thank Editorial Director Stephen Shaw of Kodansha International, copy editor Kit Pancoast Nagamura and Ichiro Ozawa of Kodansha, and the many people who gave advice and encouragement, especially Ann Flower, Josh Griffith, Marilyn Jean, Rebecca Jennison, Dana Lewis, Rebecca Lloyd-Jones, Mari Morisawa, Lucy North, Heather Willson, and Dominick Yenches and his friends at the Dave Cowens Basketball School.

Photo credits: Takao Akimoto, pp. 155, 158, 223; Hajime Sawatari, p. 156; Makoto Ayano, p. 157.

Originally published in Japan in 1998 by Kodansha Ltd. under the title *Gotai Fumanzoku*.

Distributed in the United States by Kodansha America, Inc., and in the United Kingdom and continental Europe by Kodansha Europe Ltd.

Published by Kodansha International Ltd., 17–14 Otowa 1-chome, Bunkyo-ku, Tokyo 112–8652, and Kodansha America, Inc.

ISBN-13: 978-4-7700-2764-1
ISBN-10: 4-7700-2764-8

First edition, 2000
First paperback edition, 2003
15 14 13 12 11 10 09 08 07 06   10 9 8 7 6 5 4 3 2

Library of Congress Cataloging-in-Publication Data available

www.kodansha-intl.com

Contents

3—The Barrier-Free Heart
My Time at Waseda University

Prologue

April 6, 1976. Cherry trees in full blossom, soft sunlight. A gentle day.

A baby came squalling into the world. A bouncing baby boy. It was an ordinary birth to an ordinary couple. Except for one thing: the boy had no arms or legs.

Congenital tetra-amelia: the condition of being born without arms or legs. It wasn't due to a difficult birth, or the drug thalidomide, whose harmful effects were in the news at the time. The cause in my case is still unknown. For whatever reason, I arrived with an ultra-individual appearance that startled people. How many people get a shocked reaction just by being born? Probably only Momotaro, the fairy-tale boy who was found inside a peach, and me.

A birth is supposed to be followed by the joyful moment when mother and child first see each other's faces. But my father thought over what might happen. If my mother found out right after the delivery, before she'd had any chance to recover her strength, wouldn't the shock be too much for her? As she lay in bed, he said to her, "I'm afraid you can't see the baby right away—he's a little weak."

Two or three days passed. My father resolved to keep

the facts hidden until my mother was fully recovered. It must have been a lonely struggle. It took strength.

"They say you can't see him for a little while longer because he has severe jaundice," he told her.

It's only very recently that concepts like "informed consent" have begun to be taken up in Japan. The situation back then, in 1976, was that a doctor's word was final. Even though it was their own health and happiness at stake, patients had no choice but to leave everything to their physician. And so my father took the stance that he was simply following the doctors' orders.

Although she hadn't wondered what was going on at first, naturally my mother was worried and perplexed when she still wasn't allowed to see her own child after a week. She realized something serious must have happened, but at the same time there was an atmosphere that made it hard for her to come right out and ask anything. Of course she wanted to see her son, but she sensed this "something." She put her trust in my father.

The day of our first meeting arrived at last. Three weeks had gone by since I was born. On the day before she came to see me, my mother had been told that the reason she hadn't been allowed to see her son was not because of jaundice, but because of a disability. My father couldn't bring himself to tell her the exact nature of the disability, but what he did tell her was enough for my mother. And she prepared herself.

The hospital, too, had done what it could to get ready. An empty bed had been made available in case she fainted on the spot. The tension grew, for my father and the staff, and for my mother.

The big moment arrived, but not in the way people had expected. The words that burst from my mother's lips were "He's adorable." All the fears that she might get hysterical or keel over turned out to be unnecessary. For nearly a month, she hadn't been able to see the baby she'd given birth to. The joy of seeing her child at last was greater than the shock of his missing arms and legs.

I think the success of this first encounter was especially meaningful. First impressions tend to stick. Sometimes you're still carrying them as baggage years later. And when it's a parent and child—that meeting is a profoundly important one.

The first emotion my mother felt toward me was not shock or sadness, it was joy.

At the age of three weeks, I was born at last.

The King
in the Wheelchair

My Preschool and Elementary School Years

A Little Tyrant

Napoleon

Our life as a family of three began in a place called Kasai in Edogawa Ward, on the eastern boundary of Tokyo. My parents had just moved to the area and didn't know anyone there. I've heard of parents who hide the very existence of a disabled child by keeping him shut up at home, but mine certainly didn't. They took me out and about with them all the time so the neighbors could get acquainted with me. My arms and legs are about eight inches long now, but in those days they were potato-like bumps on my torso. My resemblance to a toy bear made me an instant favorite in the neighborhood. (I've heard of "He's the cutest little doll" as a compliment for a baby, but "He's the cutest little stuffed animal," now that's a new one!)

I had already begun to exercise my talents as a problem child. I never, ever slept. I cried fiercely all through the night, despite the fact that I didn't sleep much in the daytime. My bleary-eyed mother thought she was headed for a nervous breakdown. I earned the nickname Napoleon, after the hero who is said to have commanded his troops on just three or four hours of sleep.

I also drank way too little formula—about half the right amount for my age, according to a child-care book my mother read. That just had to be too little. My usually calm parents anxiously sought the doctors' advice, but I went right on drinking the same amount. Perhaps ready to give up by this time, they tried a new approach.

"He's been highly individual ever since he was born," they decided. "So it's no wonder he needs a different amount of formula or sleep. Let's stop comparing him with other children."

That was pretty cool. And sure enough, in spite of getting so little sleep and formula, I grew rapidly and was never sick.

At nine months, I produced my first word. All I'd done till then was babble, but suddenly I went, "Happapa, happapapa, papa, papa." My mother was a little put out that my first word was "papa," but she kept telling herself that it was simply easier to say. And my parents were very happy that I'd started to talk.

From then on, they say, it was as though a dam had burst. By my first birthday I was known as Chatterbox Hiro. My father entertained himself giving me "lessons" with a set of wooden picture blocks he'd bought. He would show me one with a washing machine on it and ask, "What's this?"

"Wishwash."

"And this?"

"Papa-eye" (glasses).

"What's this, then?"

"Noothpaper."

And so forth. These classes took place every evening when my father came home from the office.

My mother, meanwhile, had seen an article in the paper that warned, "Not reading to your child amounts to giving him or her a frontal lobotomy," which prompted her to read to me in every spare moment. They were both pretty education-minded parents.

A year or so earlier, they had resigned themselves to the idea that I might spend my whole life confined to bed. Now their life—our life—was full of hope.

A Barrage of Questions

When I turned four, I started at Seibo Kindergarten. As it was on the west side of the city, to save a lot of driving back and forth we upped and moved to Yohga in Setagaya Ward, about ten minutes by car from the kindergarten. Since my first memories date from around this time, when I'm asked where I'm from, I say Yohga.

Seibo wasn't specially set up for disabled children, but the basic policy was respect for the children's individuality. There was none of the usual "What shall we all do now?" We each did whatever we wanted, within the rules. This approach was perfect for me. If we'd all had to do the same activities, there were bound to have been things I couldn't do.

I made friends at once, thanks to my arms and legs, or lack thereof. First, the other kids' attention was caught by a strange machine—my power wheelchair. When they looked closer, the rider had no arms and legs! This was a great mystery. The moment they spotted me they'd gather like a swarm of ants, touching my limbs and asking "Why, why, why?" Whenever this happened, I used to explain, "I got sick when I was in my mom's tummy, and so my arms and legs didn't grow." That was all they needed to hear, and from then on we got along fine together.

It did get tiring, though, during the month or two that it took for the explanation to reach everyone, from my class-mates to all the other children. Every day I was bombarded with questions. My mother says she remembers clearly the first time I came home whining, "I'm worn out." The teach-ers were concerned, too, as they saw what was happen-ing; they asked whether I wasn't getting a headache or a stomachache when I came home. Leaving the grown-ups to worry about such things, I went on developing into a sturdy child—and then some.

Doing It MY Way

Thanks to having short arms and legs plus a wheelchair, I was a winner in the popularity department. I found myself always the center of a circle of friends. And, little by little, the typical willfulness of an only child began to kick in.

Among preschoolers, children just a few months apart in age can be at very different stages of growth. Because my birthday, April 6, fell just after the cutoff date for enrollment, I was the oldest in my class. You might say I had leadership potential—or you could just say I was a bossy kid.

Everyone would be playing tag in the playground. This was dead boring for me, since even with my power wheelchair I couldn't keep up. So I would wheel out and yell, "If you wanna play in the sandbox, follow me!" And, strangely enough, the kids who'd been happily chasing one another a moment ago would all troop after the wheelchair to the sandbox.

Once we got there, however, I couldn't build my own sand castles without hands. And so I gave the orders. Anyone who dared to say they wanted to dig a tunnel when I'd said to make a castle was asking for trouble.

"I said we're making a castle today. If you don't like it, you can go play by yourself." Since I could already talk up a storm in those days, it seems no one was able to stand up to me.

Being so headstrong didn't lose me any friends, though. I guess they thought, "If I stay on the right side of Oto-chan* I won't be left out." This only encouraged me further. I became a real little tyrant, and gradually started getting smart with my parents and teachers as well.

While this lasted, I gave my parents a lot of headaches, they say, but there came a turning point when the problem solved itself. In my last year at kindergarten my willfulness vanished—though not, I have to admit, without a trace.

For Art Day, our class was putting on a play. The cast included "Gramps" the auto mechanic. Not a bad part, really,

* In Japan, the familiar ending *chan* is often added to a person's name (or part of it). Much like the -y or -ie in Billy or Susie, it is an endearment used by family and friends, especially with children's names.

but nobody wanted it because the name "Gramps" sounded like a grumpy old man.

Finally my best friend, Shingo, shot up his hand and said, "I'll do it, then." I thought that was a truly classy thing to do. I can still remember how pathetic it made me feel by comparison. So, not to be outdone, I put myself up for the next most unpopular part, that of the narrator. Even at six, I was probably desperate to boost my standing as a young man. I was already image-conscious in those days, I guess.

The narrator's part was voice only—in other words, I was behind the scenes. My narration went over so well that some of the mothers said, "You should become an announcer when you grow up!" For a natural-born ham like me, always hogging the spotlight, it came as a revelation that a narrator could be so well received. I started to see how much cooperation it takes from all sides—including behind the scenes—to get something done. A preschooler whose world, till then, was centered entirely on himself had just grown up a little.

After that, I discovered it was really fun to play together with other kids. I began to get along better with all my classmates; by the time we were almost out of kindergarten, I was going over to play at a friend's place practically every day.

Thus, one of the biggest problems of my preschool years was solved thanks to my being so image-conscious. But a trickier problem was waiting up ahead.

A Heavy Door

Slammed in Our Faces

I expect all parents feel a mixture of anxiety and hope when their children are about to enter the new environment of school. For the parents of a child with a disability, though, chances are the anxiety outweighs the hope. First of all, they run smack into the question, "Is there anywhere that will accept our child?"

In my case, too, this has been a problem all along. My parents were faced with the stiffest barrier of all at the entrance to elementary school. I'll bet they never dreamed they'd have so much trouble getting me a compulsory education.

Fifteen years ago, it was still taken for granted that children with disabilities would go to special schools. But these are schools for children whose educational needs differ from the mainstream. My parents weren't convinced that "regular ed" was out for me. Did this kid who fancied himself a leader and bossed everybody around at kindergarten really need special ed? They had their doubts, which grew into a desire to have me attend a mainstream school.

Their wish wasn't easily granted. They began by narrowing their sights to private elementary schools, since they thought it would be more difficult for a public school to accept a disabled child. They had also heard that private schools showed more understanding toward people with disabilities. But it was hopeless. My parents couldn't even find a school that would let me take the entrance tests. The door was slammed in our faces, so to speak.

Just when they'd half given up and begun to think I wouldn't even be given a chance to try regular ed, something came in the mail which changed the situation completely: a notice about a "Health Examination for School-Age Children." A checkup was scheduled for children due to enter elementary school the following spring, and a postcard announcing it arrived at the Ototake residence.

Amazing. It had come from the local public elementary school which my parents had ruled out from the start. Their hopes soaring, they dialed the contact number. As you'd expect, the school hadn't known that I was a child with a severe disability. The school officials seemed a little taken aback when the situation was explained to them, but even so they said, "Well, first of all, come in and see us." And so my mother took me to the checkup. This was my first encounter with Yohga Elementary School.

The "Health Examination for School-Age Children" was a zoo. A herd of lively kindergartners tearing around, kids bawling in the unfamiliar surroundings. In the midst of it all, I behaved myself as I went from one examination to the next and was even, I'm told, praised by the doctors. My mother says it gave her confidence: if I'd been praised for good behavior here, I could surely handle school.

After the last of the medical exams, we headed for the principal's office. My mother must have been very tense. The fine points of the situation were beyond my understanding at the time, but I definitely got the sense that *something* was about to happen.

My first impression of the principal was that he looked kind. He turned now and then while talking with my mother, perhaps concerned that I'd be bored, and gave me a friendly smile. After I'm not sure how long, he winked at me and asked me a question: "Is there any food you don't like?"

"Mm . . . Bread!" At the time, I didn't like that soggy feeling in my mouth.

"Really? If you don't like bread, you'll have problems with the school lunches, you know. We serve bread nearly every day."

My mother's expression, which had been stiff with tension, brightened before my eyes. He'd as good as said okay. When we got home, she reported the great news to my father: "It looks like he's going to be able to go to a mainstream school, dear."

From Heaven to Hell

Our joy was short-lived. We did receive a favorable reply from the principal, "since you live in our district," but then the local Board of Education said, "Not so fast!" The reason: there was no precedent for admitting such a severely disabled person into the regular educational system.

It was back to square one. For a while the Ototake household was stunned. There'd even been talk about school lunches. We'd thought it was a done deal, and so the setback came as all the more of a shock. But then my folks showed what they're made of. They didn't stay down for long before swinging back into action to find out what it would take to get me accepted.

There was only one thing to be done: keep on meeting with the Board of Education. The main reason they'd called this temporary halt was probably the uncertainty that came from not knowing me. And who can blame them? It must have been hard to imagine that a person with arms only four or five inches long could write as well as his peers. If we could just clear up their misgivings, permission would surely follow. That was my parents' approach.

The board members had endless questions. What did my parents do in this or that situation? My mother took me along to demonstrate in person what I could do. I remember showing off various things. Writing with the pencil held between my arm and my cheek. Eating by using the spoon or fork on the principle of a lever against the rim of the bowl. Cutting paper by taking one handle of the scissors in my mouth, steadying the other handle with my arm, and moving my head. Walking on my own by moving my short legs in turn, keeping my body in its normal L-shaped position.

Everything I did seemed to take the board members' breath away. Or perhaps I should say it mystified them. After all, here was an armless, legless person, happily carrying out all sorts of tasks one after another, right before their eyes.

In the end, my parents' enthusiasm and my own abilities won us permission to enroll. On one condition.

A typical first grader dashes out of the house with a "Bye!" in the morning, spends the day studying and playing, and announces "I'm home!" in the late afternoon. In my case, though, it was different. A guardian was required to accompany me from home in the morning, be on standby in the halls during classes and recess, and then accompany me home again. The burden on my parents would be colossal, but they were genuinely thrilled at this conditional acceptance, "if it means you can be in regular ed."

The principal and many others, by their goodwill, had opened the door for me. There was only one way to repay their kindness, and that was to enjoy school.

Takagi Sensei

No Helping

When I look at the class photo taken the day I started school, I can't help reacting with a wry smile. The girl next to me is scrooching as far away as she can get, with a kind of wince on her face. And there's me beside her with a broad grin. That picture says it all. The cause of all the fuss, the one who had everyone worrying about how he'd take to school, is beaming away without a care in the world. It seems it was the people around me who were discombobulated.

The person with the most on his mind would have been the teacher I had for first through fourth grades, Takagi Sensei. ("Sensei" is a term of respect meaning "teacher.") Takagi Sensei was such a veteran that the other teachers called him "Granddad Sensei." When my enrollment was decided, I'm told he immediately came forward and asked to have me in his class. But with all his experience, he'd never been in charge of an armless and legless child like me before. Everything was new. The first thing that troubled him was the reaction of the other children.

"Why haven't you got any arms?"

"Why are you riding in that car?"

Sometimes kids would come up to me and gingerly touch my arms and legs. Sensei says he was in a cold sweat over how to handle all this, but I was used to it. I thought of it only as a transit point on the way to becoming friends. I kept on repeating my usual explanation, "It happened in my mom's tummy."

The other children's doubts were soon cleared up, and my classmates, at least, no longer asked about my arms and legs. That took a load off Sensei's mind, but before long their growing confidence led to a new problem.

Takagi Sensei was very strict. Teachers who have children with disabilities in their class are tempted to do this and that for them, but he stopped himself since he knew it wouldn't be good for me in the long run. As the kids in my class lost their fear of me, however, an increasing number of them wanted to help me. That was especially true of the girls—perhaps they liked to think of themselves as my big sisters.

Sensei was of two minds about what was happening. On the one hand, he was pleased, since it showed a spirit of helpfulness developing in the class, along with understanding toward me. Naturally, he was reluctant to put a stop to it. On the other hand, though, he thought: If Ototake's friends help him all the time, he'll come to expect everything to be done for him while he sits back and waits.

After a struggle, Sensei announced his conclusion: "Let Ototake do the things he can do on his own. But when there's something he really can't do for himself, then you can help him." Everyone seemed disappointed, but being obedient first graders, they agreed. After that no one was in such a hurry to help me out.

Several days later, a new complication came up. There were lockers at the back of the classroom where we each kept an "arithmetic set," which held a ruler, marbles, and so on, and a "tool box," containing paste, scissors, etc. We would all go and get items from these boxes whenever they were needed for a lesson.

But I was extremely slow. When Sensei told us to fetch something, I got off to a late start because I always waited until the initial rush for the lockers was over. It would have been near suicide for me to hurl myself into the thick of it. When out of my wheelchair, as I was in the classroom, I barely came up to the other children's knees. And once I did get going, in those days it would take me quite a while to open the tool box, get an item out, replace the lid, and return to my seat.

That day, I was once again wrestling with my tool box. Normally, a child who was already done would have said, "Here, let me," and taken the item to my seat, but just last week everyone had been warned not to help me. Although they all seemed uncomfortable about it, nobody offered to help. And the lesson started up again.

Finally I burst into sobs. The first tears I'd shed at school. They weren't so much tears of frustration as tears of loneliness at being left out. Sensei rushed over.

"Good work! You did very well to get so far by yourself."

I really howled then. A comforting word can sometimes do that.

Sensei thought: He shows no resistance to being set difficult tasks, but he hates to be singled out or miss an activity. But I can't keep the whole class waiting till he finishes. And it isn't good for him to be helped with every single thing.

In this case, Sensei solved the problem by letting me use two lockers. I kept each of the boxes with its lid off in a separate locker, so there was no need to be always opening and closing boxes to get the tools out. That certainly speeded things up.

By coming up with ideas like this, Sensei took care to see that I could lead the same life at school as everyone else.

Dethroned

Whenever I went into the school yard, I was mobbed. Nobody had ever seen a child with no arms and legs before. Or a power wheelchair like mine. The two together must have been quite a novelty. Plus, it wasn't easy to see that I was steering the chair with my arms, and so it looked to the other children as though it was moving by itself.

Recess was the only time when first graders from other classes and the older kids could come in contact with me. When they caught sight of me in the playground, they gathered like ants to a piece of candy. Some asked the usual whys, others wanted a ride in the chair. Then one of my classmates would come along and explain with a knowledgeable air: "It happened when Oto-chan was in his mother's tummy, you know."

I was the center of attention of the whole school. There was always a circle around me two or three deep, and children trailed along behind me when I moved from place to place. Being the center of attention was just fine with me. Perhaps mistaking the kids who trooped after me for my loyal subjects, I crowed happily that I was "like a king."

One day, however, I found myself dethroned. By order of Takagi Sensei. "From now on," he told me, "you mustn't use your wheelchair without my permission." He had taken this drastic step for several reasons.

First, there was the sense of superiority that the chair gave me. I was very pleased with my troop of followers, but he saw through them. They weren't admirers, they were just curious about the wheelchair. In any case, the superiority complex they were giving me would undo his efforts to treat me like everyone else in order to break down the thought pattern, "people with disabilities are special."

There was also my physical strength to be considered. The grade school years are a period of rapid growth, and I would no doubt develop too, in my own way. In the wheelchair, I would have fewer chances to get my body moving. The way he saw it, looking to the future and the need to build up my muscles, the chair had no advantages and it had to go.

At the time, this was a very harsh order from my point of view. The wheelchair was, after all, my legs. Without it, as I could only walk by placing my thighs flat on the ground and shuffling my butt along, the school yard became immense. Getting around was going to take a lot of stamina.

Naturally, there was opposition. I'm told that for several

days after I began walking around the school yard there was a stream of protests (mostly from women teachers) that this was cruel. The objections grew stronger in midsummer and midwinter. When you walk with your butt flat on the ground, you feel the heat or the chill more than other people.

There was also a problem at morning assembly time in the school yard. When assembly was over, the whole school marched to music back to their classrooms. Since we lined up in order of height, small in front and tall in back, I was at the head of the boys in my class. Sensei could only tell the others to overtake me so that our class would not be left behind. This left me all alone out there and added fuel to the pro-wheelchair argument.

But still Sensei wouldn't listen. He held firm to the belief that "We can coddle him all we like right now, but he'll have to fend for himself one day. My role is to think about what we really need to do for him now for the sake of the future."

I'd say he made the right decision. The middle school, high school, and college that I went on to attend have all left something to be desired when it comes to accessibility. I've often had to park my chair at the bottom of a flight of stairs and leg it (butt it?) around campus.

I believe the mobility I have today is entirely thanks to Takagi Sensei's guidance. If I'd been using the power wheelchair all the time from those first years, I would surely have become completely reliant on it. I try to imagine what my daily life would be like . . . I'm sure it would be very different from the life I lead now in terms of freedom, mentally as well as practically.

Sensei seems to have made the conscious decision to

be strict with me. He recalls, "Even if Ototake thought I was scary, that was all right with me as long as he could later say 'But I'm glad I had him for my teacher.' "

True strictness is true kindness. When I think of Takagi Sensei, I really appreciate the meaning of these words.

The Oto-Chan Rules

What We Do with Our Hands

Day by day, there were fewer special arrangements made for me in the classroom. Not that people were any less kind or considerate, but there were no longer problems even when no one looked out for me. It was a sign that I'd become one of the class in a real sense.

In the required first-grade Japanese language textbook, there was a chapter on "What We Do with Our Hands." This was downright awkward for a teacher responsible for a child without any. As the first-grade classes reached that point in the textbook, even the other teachers were concerned about what Takagi Sensei planned to do.

"I have to admit it gave me pause, but I never thought of skipping that chapter," he says, surprisingly enough. "Being in contact with Ototake every day, I no longer had the sense that I was working with a congenital amputee. By then, I was able to treat him as one of my thirty-eight pupils." And, he adds, "I suppose I might have been reluctant to deal with that chapter if the other children, or I myself, had looked on Ototake as 'a disabled person.' "

I should explain here that the Japanese word for "hand," *te*, can also refer to the arm. (There is another word, *ude*, for "arm," but we tend to use *te* just as frequently.) At the end of the unit, Sensei asked us to write about what we had done with our hands/arms that day.

Everyone reported things like "I brushed my teeth" or "I did some writing." I put down, "I climbed onto a chair."

Strictly speaking, you don't climb onto a chair, you sit on it, and hands aren't involved. But when I sit on a chair I have to hoist myself up onto the seat, and this requires holding the chair in place with my short arms. So, I wrote, "I climbed onto a chair using my *te*."

None of the kids teased me about this. They accepted it as obvious: "It's true, when Oto-chan sits on a chair, he uses his *te*." Perhaps Sensei had such an outcome in mind when he tackled this unit.

No Holds Barred

As you can tell from my uppity attitude at kindergarten, I was pushy and I was stubborn, and as a result I clashed with my friends fairly often. Most of the time it went no farther than an argument (my specialty), but occasionally we came to blows. Before I tell you about one fight, maybe I should explain that in Japanese elementary schools, the teachers often let the kids sort out disputes among themselves without intervening. And in any case they're not in the classrooms at recess, which was when this happened.

"It was your fault, Oto-chan. Say you're sorry!"

"No! It was your fault. *You* say sorry!"

"Oh yeah? Come on up and make me, then. I dare you."

My adversary was standing on a desk, out of my reach, pulling faces. In a rage I rushed the desk and knocked it over, sending him tumbling off. Then I hurled myself at *him.*

"Hey!" he shouted. "NOW you're gonna get it!" He took a swing at me, but since his target was barely knee-high, he missed. When he switched to attacking with his feet I was a sitting duck. But there's a die-hard streak in my nature—he wasn't getting away with that.

Launching a counterattack, I grabbed his leg as he kicked at me and held on for dear life. As he struggled to break free, I hung on by the skin of my teeth. Literally.

Chomp.

"Yeowww!!"

In return for being kicked around, I'd bitten him good and hard. I must have developed a stronger jaw than most people, since I often did manual tasks with my mouth. There were distinct teeth marks on his leg. He was really hurting.

When you take someone on, you don't stop to calculate the odds. In this respect, it was no different from a "normal" fight . . . And in this corner, Hirotada "The Fangs" Ototake!?

Wanna Play?

Looking back on their schooldays, most people with disabilities say that the part of the day that hurt the most was recess—the very time that ordinary children, unless they're real bookworms, would surely say is their favorite. Why is this? Because for disabled kids the forty-five to fifty minutes of a class period pass quickly enough while they sit quietly in their seats, but during breaks, when they can't join in the fun their classmates are having, they feel a greater sense of isolation. And they can't wait for recess to be over.

Did I suffer through recess? No way. Like the other children, it was the time I looked forward to most of all. You may be wondering what a kid like me looked forward to, what kind of games I played. The fact is that I played the same games that ordinary grade-schoolers play—baseball, soccer, dodgeball, and the like. How in the world did I play baseball and soccer? Well, of course, I couldn't expect to do exactly what everyone else did. But that was no reason to give up on these games. All it took for me to be in on the action was some special rules. These were known as the Oto-Chan Rules, and they were invented by my classmates.

Baseball was my favorite. I held the bat under my arm and pivoted from the waist; this was my swing. And I could hit that ball. This was where an Oto-Chan Rule came in: When it was my turn at bat, a friend would stand by on the other side of home plate, and the moment I connected he'd take off for first base as an unorthodox pinch runner.

Another rule was written the day I slugged one to the back of the infield. For me, it was a long fly.

"Wow, Oto-chan, that's what homers are made of."

"Hey! Let's decide a home run mark for Oto-chan too."

"Yeah, good idea!"

"We get a home run when we clear the outfield, so let's make it a home run when Oto-chan clears the infield."

And so a new boundary line was drawn. Koshien Stadium, where the national high school baseball championships are played, used to feature a "Lucky Zone," made by moving the left and right outfield fences inward for the high school games. We had an "Oto-Chan Zone."

The guys came up with all sorts of rules in our other games, too. In soccer, as everybody knows, if you net a goal, you score one point. "Okay then, if Oto-chan gets a shot in, that's three points right there."

Three points in soccer is a major score. One of our players would dribble past the defenders to the goal area. As the goalie came forward, my teammate would slip a pass to me, ready and waiting. All I needed to do was take a shot on an open goal and I'd have chalked up a hat trick—three points in a single game.

The craziest rule of all was introduced in dodgeball. Namely, "If Oto-chan has the ball, several members of the other team have to come within a radius of ten feet of him." At such close range I could throw with quite a bit of force, and after a while I was able to pick off an opponent, boy or girl, with about fifty-fifty accuracy. Inside the circle, though, I didn't stand a chance of dodging, and so my position was always on the outside. If I hit one of the opposing team, someone was allowed into the circle in my place.

When the guys invented these rules, it was not in the

spirit "Let's play with the poor disabled kid." They all seem to have taken it for granted that, as one of their classmates, I would fight with them and play with them. And I took this for granted too.

My Favorite Subject Is Phys Ed

Jungle Gym-nastics

When Sensei once asked me what my favorite subject was, to his surprise I had a cocky answer: "Phys ed." I wasn't kidding, though.

Then there was the following conversation with my parents:

Me: "If I could grow either arms or legs, which do you think I want?"

Parents: "Hmm. We give up. Which do you want?"

Me: "Legs!"

Parents: "Why? If you had arms, you could do so many things for yourself."

Me: "I don't mind, because I don't have much trouble. But if I had legs, I could play soccer with the guys."

Obnoxious as it was to say I didn't have much trouble after all the things other people did to take care of me, at the time I was serious. That gives you an idea of how much I liked to be active.

Takagi Sensei, on the other hand, was in a quandary

over phys ed. How far should he go to include me, and when should he make me watch from the sidelines? His biggest worry, he remembers, was this: It's wonderful that Ototake's so willing to try everything, but there are things he just can't do. How do I persuade him to watch at those times without hurting his feelings? This conflict lasted for some time. Meanwhile, blissfully unaware of Sensei's troubles, I was up for anything.

Phys ed class began with exercises. As Sensei watched to see what I would do, I swung my short arms and bounced up and down in time with everyone's movements. "Okay," he thought, "Ototake doesn't have to do exactly the same exercise. He should do as much as he can of what everyone else is doing." Once he realized this, he says, it was easier to give me instructions.

If everyone did two laps around the track: "You go as far as that faucet and back." When they did the high jump: "We'll keep raising the bar for everyone else, but when it's your turn we'll keep lowering it. See if you can pass under it without touching." Since having to sit out the action was what I hated most, I was delighted whenever I was given a new task.

Sometimes I figured out for myself how to join in. The high bar is popular in primary school PE. It looks like the apparatus that Olympic gymnasts use to do giant swings and handstands (only theirs is eight feet high and ours was more like three or four). Both Sensei and I thought that this was one item I would have to miss, and I'd drop out of line and go over by the jungle gym, where I'd cheer the others on in their struggles.

Then it hit me: "The bottom rung of the jungle gym is just about the right height on me."

I tried gripping it under my armpits. When I clamped down, my body was lifted into the air. Looking over at the rest of the class, I saw them hard at work pulling themselves up till the bar was at their waists, then swinging their legs back and forth. And so, gripping my bar, I tried kicking off against the ground. Wham—my body flew forward, then the rebound pulled me back. By repeating this, I could swing like a pendulum. From a jungle gym—ta da!—a gymnast's high bar.

Up, Up, and Away

In January, when the class started jump-rope, Takagi Sensei's woes began again: how to include me? Although I'd been having a blast in phys ed so far, once the others started jumping rope I would get depressed every time PE came around. The funny thing is, in the end I was calling out to my friends, "Hey, c'mon and jump rope."

One day, Sensei placed me between two of my friends who were turning a rope and told me, "Now when it comes, jump the way you do in the exercises." I tried several times, but it was no good. Just as Sensei himself was about to give up, the timing clicked and I managed to clear the rope just once. I wouldn't call it a jump, exactly; it was more like I made it just far enough off the ground for the rope to pass under me. All the same, Sensei was generous with his praise: "That's terrific, Ototake. Keep going! Watch your timing. Up, up!" I waited for the rope, chanting "Up, up" under my breath to get the timing right. Now I made it over three or four times.

That was my limit, though. It took a good deal of strength to launch my whole body off the ground by springing on my short legs. It wasn't like me to whine, even when Sensei asked if I was tired, but after jumping rope I was always wiped out.

And yet, what a difference practice can make.

"Sensei, I can jump rope twenty-three times."

"Really? How did you manage that?"

"I do it with Miya-chan. Watch, Sensei."

My partner took up her position facing me, holding our rope at the ready. At the signal "Get set, go!" it started twirling. I had to jump, of course, but it'd be a no-go if my partner tripped, which was why I'd asked an expert skipper like Miya-chan to practice with me.

Up, up, and away. You could tell we'd been practicing. We were in perfect unison.

"Bravo, both of you! Keep up the good work and see if you can get past thirty."

We buckled down to more practice. A skip, and a short rest. Another attempt, another rest. I don't know how Miya-chan put up with such leisurely training sessions.

Thirty-four times. Our best yet. It might have been my imagination, but even Miya-chan seemed proud when she said, "Shall we show Sensei?" We went and found him to demonstrate the results of our intensive training. Perhaps because we were tense, we only managed twenty-nine.

Still, Sensei was beaming as he said, "Well done!" Thanks to Miya-chan, I had umpteen times more fun than the other kids jumping rope.

Hakone, Here We Come!

Around the same time that we started jump-rope, something called a "marathon card" was handed out during PE. It was a route map of the famous Tokyo–Hakone long-distance relay race. Each time we ran the "marathon" (once around the school grounds), we got to color in one more stage on our maps.

This was another of those occasions when Sensei worried about how to include me. After thinking it over for several days, he made a proposition to the class: "How would it be if Ototake colors in four stages when he runs one lap?"

"Okaaay," they chorused.

"Ototake, will that work for you too?"

"Yes, I'll run every morning."

You could say that Sensei had thought up an Oto-Chan Rule. This way I could run the marathon too without falling far behind in my coloring progress. I was raring to go.

The next day, I was Hakone-bound. The earlier I arrived at school in the morning, the more time I had to run. I took to nagging my mother to hurry up as we got ready to leave. But there was a worried look on Takagi Sensei's face as he watched me run.

Normally, being acutely sensitive to danger, I would never go near a crowd. I was such a stickler about this that, no matter how hot the weather or how thirsty I was, I would do without a drink if there was a bunch of people around the drinking fountain. In the marathon, though, we all followed the same route around the school. Since I run by shuffling my butt along in a sitting position, it would be hard for kids coming up from behind to see me. I had to be especially alert for those who were talking as they ran. The taller the kids—like the boys in the senior grades—the less likely they would be to notice me. Takagi Sensei was concerned that I might accidentally be sent flying.

As it turned out, though, he needn't have feared, because some of the older boys—sixth graders, no less—were worried about the same thing, and they ran with me. Since the pace didn't even amount to jogging for them, they took turns doing their own laps for the day, then circled back when they'd finished for a changing of the guard. So that other kids wouldn't kick me by mistake, the sixth graders gave me an escort on all four sides.

A recent heavy snow had left muddy patches in the playground along the route. They swept me up and over these, saying, "You'll get your butt wet." They were a real running bodyguard team. Like me, Takagi Sensei was delighted.

Through this combination of Sensei's ideas, my classmates' cooperation, and the older students' thoughtfulness, I was able to enjoy phys ed without ever feeling discouraged.

Sensei told me later that when he proposed the Four Stages Per Lap Rule, he was afraid that other children who weren't good at running might object. But, as I've said, the whole class agreed. We'd spent the better part of a year together by then, and they had all come to understand me. They knew, "If you give him a head start, Oto-chan can do whatever we're doing."

In fact, it may well have been Takagi Sensei who was taught this. Because it was the kids who invented the original Oto-Chan Rules.

The Taste of Rice Balls 🍎

Hey, That's Cheating!

I always looked forward to our school trips, which happened twice a year. Part of the fun, of course, was going on an outing with my friends, but an added thrill for me was the train ride. Since my family mostly used the car when we went out, I rarely had a chance to take the train. And so a school trip—getting to go on an expedition with Sensei and my friends *and* to ride the train—was the best treat ever.

In the lower grades, our excursions to nearby parks and zoos were easy enough in a wheelchair. But each year the programs were becoming a little more demanding. And with the upcoming fourth-grade trip, the pinnacle of difficulty lay ahead.

We heard the news as soon as school went back in the spring: "For our next outing, we're going to climb a mountain." What's more, we were told, it was a tough climb even for an adult. And—the words formed themselves in my head —even tougher in a wheelchair . . . This time, I thought, no matter how much I wanted to be in on everything, there was no way I could go. I'd have to get my mother to tell Sensei that I would miss the trip.

But Sensei wouldn't hear of it. "I'm sure it'll work out once we get there," he told my mother. "Especially since it wouldn't do to leave him behind halfway up."

When Sensei went on the teachers' reconnaissance trip, however, the seriousness of the situation hit him. It was one steep mountain. For longer trips like these outings, I've always used a lightweight, collapsible manual wheelchair instead of the power chair, which is heavy and tricky to maneuver. But even with the lighter chair, some of the teachers doubted that we could make it. I heard they carried on a discussion all along the trail: "We'll never get the wheelchair up here," "We might manage it on a slope like this," and so on.

Strictly speaking, the reconnaissance party was supposed to do things like locating toilets, choosing rest spots, and making sure there was an area where everyone could be marshaled into line. But before they knew it, even the teachers of the other fourth-grade classes had joined in exploring one thing: "How do we go about bringing Ototake with us?" Room 4's teacher, a big man, offered: "I'll carry him on my back if it comes to that. Bring him along and don't worry." One way or another, it seems, the entire fourth grade had braced themselves to take me with them to the top.

The next week, there was a class meeting. A weird class meeting: the topic was "What to do about Oto-chan?"

Sensei: "For our school trip, we're going to Mount Kobo in Kanagawa Prefecture. We'll be climbing the mountain. All right, everybody?"

Class: "All riiiight!"

Sensei: "I've just been there with the other teachers, and the going's really tough. What do you think? Still all right?"

Class: "All riiiight!"

Sensei: "But remember Ototake is in a wheelchair. The other day, his mother told me he won't be coming on the trip this time. What do you think?"

One of the class: "Hey, that's cheating!"

This was such an unexpected reply that Takagi Sensei couldn't hide his surprise.

One of the class: "If it's such a tough mountain to climb, it's not fair that only Oto-chan gets out of going!"

Cries of "That's right!" went up from the other kids.

They were the ones who would have to work extra hard if I went. It meant taking a wheelchair up a peak that was difficult enough to begin with.

And yet, what they came out with was "It's not fair that only Oto-chan gets out of going!" It just didn't make sense to them that this one member of the class be excused from an event. Which is how I, too, came to challenge Mount Kobo.

Teamwork

The heavens didn't smile on us. It poured on the morning of the big day. The plan in case of wet weather was to postpone the trip to the next day—so the downpour meant that, even if the next day turned out perfect, we would have to hike up a muddy trail.

On account of the rain, also, we lost the backup we'd been counting on. Ordinarily my mother would accompany me on class trips, but for the climb my father, being stronger, had arranged to take the day off from work. The following day, however, he was scheduled to go to Nagasaki on business, and there was no way he could take the time off.

With so much at stake, it rained. The fact that it cleared up by noon, turning into quite a nice day, only made me resent the early morning downpour all the more.

The weather stayed fine for the outing a day later. But there stood the mighty Mount Kobo, looming above us as if to say, "Climb me? Hah!" Even Sensei, who'd said, "I'm sure it'll work out once we get there," admits that suddenly he didn't feel so sure of reaching the top. As for me, I was worried half out of my mind: up *there* in a wheelchair? Was that possible? Mount Kobo looked so formidable, you had to wonder.

As soon as we set off, the trail headed steeply uphill for about five to ten minutes. It was not only steep but very narrow, and the ground was soft after the rain. There were spots where the tires of my wheelchair nearly got stuck. When the chair was simply pushed, we didn't make much headway. The front wheels had to be lifted and the chair half-carried up the slope at a rush. The next thing I knew, even the vice principal was lending a hand.

This wasn't an encouraging start. Could we really make it all the way to the top? Never having done any mountain-climbing before, I was knocked for a loop by that first slope. It looked like it ought to be named The Heart-Stopper, and my own heart felt ready to burst with anxiety.

For a while after that, apart from some ups and downs, the going was fairly easy compared to that first precipitous part. Since Takagi Sensei is not especially strong himself, he saved his strength for the really rough places and left the level stretches of the trail to the children.

By fourth grade, some boys are pretty big. Daisuke and Shin, who were the biggest and strongest in the class, took charge of the chair. But big as they were, we're talking about the strength of ten-year-olds. On the bumpy trail, progress was slow with just the two of them pushing. We needed someone to go around and lift the front wheels when they bogged down, and clear stones and twigs out of the way. That role was taken on by some of the smaller kids who were quick off the mark.

Miya-chan took up a position on my right, Takayuki on my left, and when the wheels hit a snag they whisked them up and over. The two of them were in perfect sync. When the path steepened, Takagi Sensei and the other teachers took over pushing and we charged uphill. It was great teamwork.

Everyone was red in the face. Their necks were soaked with sweat, and because of the mushy ground they had mud up to their knees. "All-out" doesn't begin to describe the effort they were putting in for me.

I was choked up with a mixture of gratitude and wanting to apologize to everyone. This, plus the frustration of not being able to do anything myself, left me not even knowing what to say. I wished I could jump down and join in pushing the chair from behind. But since that wasn't about to happen, I just prayed and prayed that we'd reach the top any moment now.

It was a long way to the top. It felt as if we'd been walking for three days already. But, at last, light appeared through the trees up ahead. Everybody put on a burst of speed. The last spurt brought us to the summit, and all at once the view spread out before our eyes. We had conquered Mount Kobo.

"We did it!!"

"Sensei, look, look!"

"Wow!"

Shouts of excitement went up here and there. Some kids sprawled on the ground. Some drained their water bottles without stopping for breath. Some came over to shake hands and say, "We did it, hey, Oto-chan?" Whatever they were doing, they all had a great look on their faces.

I knew I ought to go around and thank them, but I was worn out myself. For some reason I was too limp to move. I guess I must have been really pumped up in the wheelchair. Which goes to show I was with everyone in spirit.

If I were asked, "What's the best food you've ever tasted?" it would be a cinch: "The rice balls I ate at the top of Mount Kobo."

The V Sign on My Back

The Nightmare Returns

In the locker rooms at school, for example, or when I'm away from home and someone helps me take a bath, most people have caught their breath when they see my back. They're struck by the painful-looking scars which run from my shoulders to the small of my back, as if someone had painted on a big letter V. These are the marks of a series of operations I went through in fourth grade.

I had my first operation while in kindergarten. Since bones grow faster than soft tissue, if something hadn't been done the bones of my arms would have burst through the flesh and popped out the ends. Running sores did in fact begin to develop at the tips of my arms when I was five, and it was decided to operate.

The surgeon took some bone from my hip and inserted it in wedges at the ends of my arm bones to prevent further growth. Being so young at the time I don't have much memory of all this, but my parents remember it only too clearly. The strain of watching me go into the operating room. The seemingly endless wait for the surgery to end. And the months I spent encased in plaster casts in a hospital bed. They didn't ever want to go through that again.

It wasn't over, however. The year I turned ten, changes started to occur in my arms. Where they'd been as round as potatoes, they gradually became pointed. At first, I didn't let it bother me. But after a while I couldn't ignore it because the ends began to hurt.

It was a stabbing pain like nothing I'd ever known. We went to the hospital and had X rays taken, and sure enough, we were told that the bones were trying to push their way through again. I had entered a growth period and my bones were developing fast.

It hurt worse every day. Just the touch of my clothes brushing against my arms when I was changing would send sharp pains shooting up them. I was given special permission not to change for PE, but I must have really loved that class, because even with my arms hurting so badly it was the only one I never wanted to miss.

Soon, however, the problem began to interfere even with PE and playtime. First, I could no longer play my favorite ball games. There was no way I could handle a ball when even the touch of clothing against my arms was acutely painful. In the end, I couldn't even run. Because I run with a kind of hopping motion on my butt, my whole body moves up and down, and the jolt each time I landed made my arms throb. It felt as if wires were being driven into me and twisted around.

Since being active was such a big part of my life, it was slow torture to lose the things I could do, one by one. Finally, the situation we'd been dreading arose. The tips began to fester. A new round of surgery was decided on. It was scheduled for my fourth-grade summer vacation.

The Surgeon Is Ready (I'm Not)

My having no arms or legs gave the doctors all sorts of logistical problems in preparing for the surgery. First, there was the general anesthetic. Being small, apparently I require a different amount of anesthetic from other people. Since even a slight error in the dose can cause a serious accident, the anesthesiologist had a nerve-racking time.

Next, the blood samples and IVs. Ordinarily, I'm told, it's easiest to insert the needle into one of the blood vessels in the arms, but on me they're not there. The doctor stood with his arms folded, deep in thought. Then he had a bright idea which made me turn pale.

"I've got it. Remember when I took your pulse, I put my hand on your neck?"

That's right. He'd decided to use a neck vein to draw blood and put in the IVs. This was one thing I would never get used to. The needle comes in right next to your face. No matter how many times it was done, I was scared to death.

On a hot midsummer's day—my fifth day in the hospital, but all too soon for me—it was time for the surgery. Somehow none of it seemed real until, with several hours to go, I had to put on that cloth thing they called a hospital gown. I thought, with a wrench, "It's happening." Anxiety washed over me in waves.

This operation would be different from the last. Muscle tissue taken from my back would be grafted onto my left arm, wrapping around the tip. The idea was that muscle, which grows faster than the other soft tissues, would be able to keep pace with the bone.

I was placed on the kind of stretcher on wheels that I'd often seen on TV, and was on my way to the operating room. Tears threatened to spill over when I parted from my parents, but I squeezed them back; it wouldn't look good to cry. Thinking about it now, I'm impressed that I could worry about something like that. But after I was wheeled past my parents and the doors flapped shut, a single tear trickled down my cheek. For all my show of toughness, I was still a ten-year-old. I was scared.

Sensing this, a nurse spoke to me. "Are you scared of the operation?"

"Mm."

"Everything will be all right. As soon as you get into the operating room they'll give you some medicine to make you go to sleep, and when you wake up it'll all be over. You won't feel a thing."

Just as she'd said, I was put under at once. As I lost consciousness, I felt the world spinning away from me, or me being sucked away somewhere. For some reason, a conversation between a nurse and a doctor that was going on right beside me is firmly fixed in my memory.

"How old is your son now, Doctor?"

"Mine? He's thirteen. Already in middle school."

"Is he as big as that already? What was his name again?"

"Ryutaro. Lately he's started complaining that it's got such complicated characters in it, in an exam it takes him way too long to wri—"

When I came to, it was evening. The operation had taken longer than the scheduled three hours. It was, as far as they could tell, a success.

The Blues

In that particular hospital, unlike some where a family member can stay and help take care of the patient around the clock, the nurses did everything, and visitors—even parents —were only allowed between 3:00 and 7:00 P.M. The day of the operation was no exception; at seven o'clock both my parents had to leave. "We'll take care of him now," they were told. "Please go on home."

I was too woozy after the surgery to care, but as one day passed and then another, I grew more and more lonely. As seven o'clock rolled around, I would kick up a fuss when I heard that my parents had to go, putting them on the spot by pleading, "Stay another minute." My mother remembers how hard it was to tear herself away.

The loneliness was partly due to my feeling weak after the operation, of course, but the main reason was my contact with the other kids—or lack of it. I wasn't ignored or picked on, but this was a hospital. Patients came and went all the time, and even if I got to know someone a little, they soon checked out. In the orthopedic ward where I was, many children came in for things like broken bones, and their stays were short. For a long-term patient like me, it certainly wasn't an easy place to make friends.

And, it mustn't be forgotten, there was my disability. I don't mean to say that disabled people can't make friends. But nothing could have been farther from the minds of the other children, they were so startled at seeing me for the first time. I was sure I could make friends if only they had a chance to get used to me, like the kids at school, but there wasn't time for that. They all left before we got to know each other.

Another thing making me miserable was that the hospital—perhaps afraid of shrieking youngsters tearing around —had a rule that barred visitors under the age of fourteen. Some of my friends wanted to visit, but that never came about. Since playing with them was my chief purpose and pleasure in life, not seeing them for nearly two months was as lonely as being plunked down in the middle of a vast desert.

Under these conditions, my usual high spirits vanished during my stay in the hospital. I was very discouraged. One day, a nurse who noticed me moping stopped for a chat. I'd gone for so long with hardly anyone to talk to that I talked and talked. I told her about the operation, my school, life in the hospital, my favorite cartoon shows, and how lonely I was.

She listened with a twinkling smile from beginning to end, and when I'd finished she put her hand gently on my shoulder. How long since I'd felt such warmth? That faint glow from my shoulder made me feel secure, and the tension snapped. Giving way to all the tears I'd been holding back, I burst into loud wails.

"I want to go home."

I was in a state where a small act of kindness touched me deeply. I felt the warmth of a caring gesture. I'd never been very appreciative of all that my friends and teachers did for me, and this episode may have taught me a lesson.

Takagi Sensei, who was hearing reports of how I was doing from my mother, says he could hardly stand it. When school started he proposed to the class that they all write me a letter. Their replies took him completely by surprise.

"Sensei, I've been passing around an exercise book and getting everyone to write a few lines."

"We're folding paper cranes. We're going to make a thousand cranes between the two of us."

"Yesterday I took some candies to the Ototakes' house for him to eat in the hospital."

For the rest of my stay, I had everyone's good wishes to keep my spirits up.

The two months passed. The stitches were taken out and the plaster came off. I gazed fearfully at my back in the mirror. The scar extended from the tip of my arm, passed under my armpit, and ran crosswise down my back like the slash of a sword.

My father said, "You know, you'll be having the operation on your right arm during winter vacation, Hiro. Then you'll have the same scar on the other side, too. It'll make a V. V for Victory."

Instead of being hard to bear, that scar began to seem more like a medal.

Otohiro Printing Inc.

Oka Sensei

In the fifth grade, we got a new teacher. He was still in his twenties, a strapping five-foot-eleven former college football player. He was the one who had offered to carry me on his back on our hike up Mount Kobo. Being close to his students in age helped him understand the way we felt, and he was extremely popular.

When I entered Yohga Elementary School, two teachers had asked to have me in their class. One was Takagi Sensei, the other was my new teacher, Oka Sensei. At that time Oka Sensei was still a "freshman" himself and the principal decided he was too young to take on a child who required special attention. But when Takagi Sensei retired, Oka Sensei, as the other candidate, agreed to take over.

I was a little tense about beginning the fifth grade with a new teacher. We started with a big cleanup (a regular part of school life in Japan). I was holding a cleaning rag under my leg, the way I always did, and wiping the floor. Since I couldn't hold it with my arms, I couldn't wipe walls or desks, which left only the floor. Even then I could only use a dry cloth; with a wet one, the legs and seat of my pants would get soaked. Seeing me doing this for the first time, Oka Sensei asked me to come to the teachers' room. "We need to have a talk," he said.

Wondering what was up—was I in trouble all of a sudden?—I followed behind him. When we arrived at his desk, he plunked himself down on the floor. The height difference of three feet or so shrank and we were on the same eye level at last. It was the first time I'd talked with him man to man.

The Strange Contraption

Sensei took some sort of machine from his desk and placed it on the floor in front of me. It was a word processor.

"The cleaning jobs everyone does are a problem for you, aren't they?"

"Mm."

"And there are other things you can't do without someone to help you, aren't there?"

"Mm."

"Well, how'd you like to do your share for the class using this?"

In a sense, this was the opposite of Takagi Sensei's approach. Instead of opting for no special treatment, for having me do what everyone else did as far as I could, Oka Sensei took the attitude, "If he can't do the same things, we'll find a trade-off." More than a difference in approach was involved here, I think. Oka Sensei was probably allowing for the fact that, as my classmates developed physically by leaps and bounds, there were going to be fewer and fewer things that I could do just like the others.

He was also aware of the fact that, in day-to-day school life, there were sure to be lots of things that I would need to ask him or my classmates to help me with. No doubt they would be happy to help. But how would I feel about having to ask all the time? What if I ended up feeling wimpy and helpless? He wanted to give me a job that only I could do, so that at times when I might start feeling small I could say, holding my head high, "But I do *this* for everyone." That inspired him to put me in charge of the word processor as my contribution to the class.

The words "I'll do it" were out of my mouth before I had time to think whether I could operate the keyboard with my arms or master the machine (not exactly being a whiz with technology). No eleven-year-old could have resisted this strange contraption that made letters and characters appear when you tapped its keys.

The next day, Sensei launched Otohiro Printing Inc.— a contraction of my name, which in the Japanese order (surname first) is Ototake Hirotada. The logo was neatly lettered on a big manila envelope. "You're the president. Go for it," he said as he handed me the envelope, which would be used for receiving and delivering orders.

The Secretary

I was enthralled by the word processor. Partly because it was fun to fool around with, but more because I felt I had a mission: "Sensei has trusted me with this huge job. I've got to learn it quickly so I can be useful to him."

It didn't take too long before I could type up a draft that Sensei had dashed off in longhand, lay it out, and produce a decorative printout. Each day there were more opportunities for "Otohiro products" to make their debut in the classroom—notices for the bulletin board, handouts, details of class trips, etc.

It seems my job performance exceeded Sensei's expectations. After a while I started receiving orders from other teachers as well as the music, art, and home ec departments. Perhaps, without my knowing, Oka Sensei had been bragging, "Well, I do have an efficient secretary, you know."

Looking back, I wouldn't be surprised to find I was working harder than the kids with the cleaning chores. But I was having so much fun with the word processor that I didn't care. In fact, I reveled in the astonished looks I got the first time I delivered the finished goods to teachers who, when they placed their orders, had only half believed that a limbless child could really do the job. And then there were the cries from my classmates: "Wow! Did you make this, Oto?"

Oka Sensei must have been anxious at first. I expect he worried whether he was doing the right thing in deciding from the start that certain things were beyond me and giving me a different task. I might have taken it as discrimination.

He also risked planting the notion that "Ototake is special" in the other children's heads. But he took those chances.

Underlying his decision there was probably the idea, "We must make a clear distinction between what he can and can't do." This becomes very important when a person with a disability goes out into the world and chooses an occupation. In giving me an education which looked not just to the present but far into the future, he was no different from Takagi Sensei.

The Otohiro Printing envelope was worn to tatters by all its comings and goings. I still have it carefully put away.

The Early Morning Runners

My First Race

Since Yohga held its Sports Day (a kind of combination festival and track meet) in May, we'd no sooner begun the new school year than we started rehearsing. Until now, I had sat out the running races. I did take part, somehow, in things like dancing. I also joined in the game where teams compete to toss the most balls into a basket at the top of a pole. Since I couldn't throw high enough, it was my job to gather the balls that fell on the ground and pass them to my classmates.

As the one thing I really hated at school was being left out, I didn't like Sports Day much, to tell the truth. And to make matters worse, we were seated in sections by grade; when it was our turn to perform, I couldn't bear having to cheer everyone on from the empty bleachers.

And now my fifth Sports Day was approaching. One day, Oka Sensei came to me with an idea. When he asked, "What will you do this year?" I didn't know what he meant at first. Then he added, "Would you like to run in a race?"

He may have been encouraged to let me take part by

the fact that I'd grown quite strong. I broke into a delighted grin. "I'll run," I said.

But it would take me at least two minutes to run a hundred meters. Even the slowest of the other kids took about twenty seconds. And so Sensei proposed, "How about if you start from halfway, Hiro? From the fifty-meter mark?" It bothered me a little, but since I wasn't confident about running the whole distance, I agreed.

I admire his courage. One reason why I hadn't been able to take part in track events before now was this: there was no guarantee that some of the spectators wouldn't take one look at me shuffling my butt and say, "Why are they making a child like that run in front of everybody? The poor boy. It's very insensitive of the school." To my mind, it's this attitude that is discriminatory, but perhaps it's inevitable in Japan, where people tend to think "poor fellow" when they see a disabled person. But Oka Sensei didn't yield an inch to that way of thinking. As he saw it, "It's not the spectators' feelings that count."

My Best Friend

I was great pals with a boy in my class named Minoru, who lived nearby. He was a really nice kid. After we entered fifth grade he gave me practically all the personal help I needed. He was also a first-rate baby-sitter on whom the neighborhood mothers depended. He had simple honesty written all over him.

Like many Japanese elementary schools, Yohga required

students who walked to school from the same area to come in a group. There were no sixth graders on our block, and so, though only a fifth grader, it was steady, responsible Minoru who was asked to lead us.

I'm reminded of something that happened in our last year at middle school. That autumn, practice interviews were held to help students prepare to apply to private high schools. We all had to do one, whether we were applying or not.

The principal, playing interviewer, asked me to name a person I respected. A model answer would have been along the lines of "my parents," or a historical figure like Hideyo Noguchi, the bacteriologist, or Helen Keller. However, I hadn't worked on my interview skills because I wasn't trying for a private school, and I was stuck. After a pause, I hit on an answer:

"My classmate Minoru."

The principal was obviously surprised. "Hm . . . why is that?"

"You may not know, sir, but he's a wonderful person. People our age tend to be wrapped up in their own problems, but he's able to think of others first, and I respect him for it."

At the end of the interview, the principal said, "I know what you mean about your friend. He's a fine young man with a kind heart."

I don't want to give the impression that Minoru was a boring straight-arrow kind of guy, though. We used to hang out and do dumb things together.

We hung out in a threesome (people called us "the Terrible Trio") with another classmate who lived in the apartment building opposite mine. He was a different type from

Minoru: assertive, a born leader and attention-getter, a big man in class who ran for every committee. He plunged right into everything at full tilt. One day, he brought us an interesting proposal.

"They say there's gobs of money dropped on the ground the day after the shrine fair." I'd never heard of this, but he could be onto something. "We'll have to get up early, though," he continued, "to beat the rush." Listening to him, Minoru and I began to get a gleam in our eyes, and before we knew it we'd planned a scavenger hunt for the day after the fair.

The carnival was over. There we were at 6:30 A.M., sitting in a row on the stone steps of Yohga Shrine with Cokes and long faces.

"So where's all the money?"

"The shrine guys must have got it when they swept up at dawn."

"There was nothing but bottle caps. We're out the price of these Cokes."

Even as we grumbled, I was happy. We may not have found any money, but I was so happy to have these buddies to do dumb things with that I didn't care. It was good just knowing they were there.

But to get back to Sports Day. When I was given the chance to take part in the race, my vanity wouldn't allow me to look like a klutz in front of all those people. When you run by dragging your butt there's no way you can do it with style, but even at that age, I guess, the need to look good was a factor.

I must have read too many comic books about aspiring boxers, because my first thought was "Early morning training!" I'd never tried to run fifty meters nonstop before, but I figured I should be able to go the distance if I built up my stamina by running first thing every morning.

Since Minoru lived nearby, I invited him along for moral support. Two or three weeks before Sports Day we began our crash training program, meeting at 6:30 for a run around the block. This took me half an hour. Except when it rained, we went out every day.

I was brimming with confidence. With all the training I'd put in, I was sure I could do myself credit when it came to the real thing. By now I could hardly wait for the race, and I didn't mind getting up at the crack of dawn day after day.

For Minoru, though, these "runs" were barely walking speed, plus there were rest stops. It was no training for him —it was more like an early morning stroll around the block. Yet he never looked reluctant and never once complained. When I arrived at our meeting place at 6:30, he would be standing there waiting for me as if it were nothing special. Smiling as usual.

My Debut

The big day arrived. The weather couldn't have been better —gentle May sunshine in a cloudless sky. Long before the hour of the fifth grade's hundred meters, my heart was hammering with excitement at my Sports Day debut. And then it was my turn. When a line was drawn at the fifty-meter mark, there was a look on people's faces that said "Huh?" I trotted out to take my mark. There was a buzz among the crowd. I felt kind of like a star.

At the sound of the pistol we were off. The other five runners closed the gap in the blink of an eye and left me in the dust as we rounded the curve. As I've said, even the slow kids could do the hundred meters in under twenty seconds. In other words, after twenty seconds there was no one but me on the track. It was a one-man show. I could hear shouts of "Go! Go!" amid the applause that was gradually swelling. It made me a bit self-conscious, but I still enjoyed it.

Coming into the last ten meters, though, I was pooped out and slowing down. At that moment, Oka Sensei's voice rang out: "Don't rest, run!" My joy at being in the race suddenly came back to me and gave me a final burst of strength.

I crossed the finish line over twenty seconds behind the others. But I felt an enormous sense of fulfillment at having gotten there. To the applause of the crowd, I lined up behind the banner that read "6th." I was probably the only child in sixth place who looked as thrilled as if he'd won first prize.

Before I went home, Oka Sensei asked, "Will you be running again next year?"

Like a shot, I answered, "Yes sir!"

Kanji Champion 🖊

For Extra Credit

Oka Sensei was a famous "idea man." He reserved the seat nearest the door for wrongdoers to sit and think things over; it was known as Devil's Island. When you left something at home, the rule was that you had to write out line after line of kanji (the Chinese characters used in the Japanese writing system), but he also provided a way out: "Kanji Passes" were issued for good behavior, and by handing one over you could escape the drill when you'd forgotten something. His most cunning invention, though, was the way he designed his kanji tests, which worked like a charm on me.

The unusual thing about these tests was how they were scored. In a regular kanji test, you're given a phrase containing a word that is written phonetically, and you have to fill in the right characters to match that pronunciation and correctly complete the phrase. For example, when you're given "to __?__ the interior of a store," plus the pronunciation *kaisō*, you fill in 改装 (remodel). This much was also true of Oka Sensei's tests, but then below each question there was a space for writing down all the homonyms you could think of for extra credit—all the words pronounced the same way but written differently and having different meanings. In the case of *kaisō*, ten bonus points would be awarded for 階層 (stratum) and another ten for 回想 (reminiscence).

Thus, the maximum possible score on a test was not 100 percent. Scores of 150 or 200 were common. Everyone pulled out all the stops, since the harder you tried the more points you could earn. For example, *kansō*: 感想 (impressions), 乾燥 (drying), 歓送 (send-off), 間奏 (interlude), 完走 (finishing a race) . . .

Sensei had his work cut out for him grading our papers, as some of the kids would go to any lengths, coming up with things like company names. He found himself constantly checking the dictionary to make sure there really was such a word. It took forever to mark the questions that gave us free rein, rain, reign.

The student with the top total score after five tests was declared class champion. That was me every time. Since I spent more of the after-school hours at home than the other kids, the kanji championship, with all the painstaking dictionary work it required, was right up my alley. Another incentive was the fact that, by nature, I hate to lose.

There were two parts to the competition: first finding words and then memorizing them. But my dictionary didn't list enough compound words to give me an edge. Then an ad in the newspaper caught my eye, and it was love at first sight. That treasure trove of a dictionary, *Daijirin*, must have been at least four inches thick. At the thought of all the compounds it would contain, I sighed as though I were gazing at a juicy steak in a restaurant.

But it carried a hefty price tag. At ¥5,800 (about US$20 at the time), it was out of the reach of a grade-schooler like me. Yet the goddess of kanji hadn't forsaken me. As luck would have it, it was December and the air was turning frosty—Christmas was just around the corner. When my grandmother inquired, "Hiro-chan, what do you want for Christmas this year?" I was ready. "*Daijirin!*" I must have come off as a very studious grandchild, but to me the kanji tests were like a game. The thick dictionary I was clamoring for was more like an expensive toy in my eyes than a study aid.

And once that toy was mine, my standing in the kanji tests would be rock-solid.

One Thing Nobody Can Beat Me At

Although I held on to the title, my position was under constant threat from a rival who always came in second. She was the brightest kid in the class. She was usually amiable and quiet—the type who spent recess reading a book in the classroom—but when she did speak out, it was with a boldness that was unexpected in a girl. Even the boys were afraid of her.

One day, she declared war. "You've beaten me for the last time, Oto, got it?" Oka Sensei had evidently put her up to this by telling her that she shouldn't let me go on acting like a big shot forever (or words to that effect).

Like a true die-hard, I took her up on it. "I'm going to

be the champion next time, too."

"Oh no you're not. I'm telling you, I can beat you at anything."

"There's one thing nobody can beat me at."

"What? If it's to do with school work, I'm as good as you."

"No, that's not it."

"What is it, then?"

"It's having no arms or legs."

I wasn't just saying this to get back at her. I was *me* because I had no arms and legs. And nobody else could be me. Though still a child, I was perhaps beginning in this way to take pride in who I was.

In Japanese class we had recently learned the difference between two words that are both pronounced *tokuchō*. There's 特徴 which means "a distinctive feature," while 特長 means "a distinctive merit or strong point." In other words, the first simply refers to a difference, while the second refers to an excellent difference.

When we were set such topics as "Introducing Myself," I used to write, "Distinguishing Feature: Having no arms or legs," but from the day of that lesson, I remember, I took to writing the kanji for "Strong Point" instead.

Maybe there aren't too many people who could have understood what I meant when I said, "There's one thing nobody can beat me at. It's having no arms or legs." But she did seem to understand, after she'd thought about it for a while.

The Super Kickboard

Fear of Water

In the summer of sixth grade, we faced the distance swimming meet. The aim was for every sixth grader to swim twenty-five meters. That included me. But getting there was a long haul.

To go back to June of my first-grade year: In the two months since I started school, Takagi Sensei had run into one new problem after another—PE, a class trip, Sports Day—and cleared those hurdles one by one. The wall that lay ahead of him now was swimming.

At the time, I was just over two foot three. The pool, at more than three feet deep, was way over my head. Which meant I couldn't go in by myself.

And so Takagi Sensei pondered—not whether to have me sit the lessons out, but how to get me into the pool. His solution was to wade into the water himself with me in his arms. This was really going overboard, when you think of the stamina it required, and the principal worried that he was taking on too much and would wear himself out. But

Takagi Sensei insisted that it was what the teacher in charge should do.

When it was decided to include me in swimming classes, I was half excited, half afraid. As I've mentioned, I've always had a keen sense of danger, ever since I was little. I would never go near a crowd of children in the school yard; no matter how thirsty I might be, I would do without a drink if there were people jostling around the drinking fountain. As for going into a pool where I couldn't touch the bottom, that was as dangerous as it gets. The fact that, with my round arms like potatoes, I couldn't wipe my face if it got wet may have contributed to my fear of water. In any case, I was filled with equal parts of delight at being able to go in with everybody else and terror of the pool.

On opening day, Sensei and I had a promise that we would go into the pool together, but in the end I balked. I changed into swimming trunks and got as far as the side, but I was too scared. He stood in the water, beckoning and coaxing: "Come on in and join us, just for a little while," but I kept going "No! No!" to the very end.

Sensei understood my fear very well, but he was determined to get me into the pool. His idea was to have me progress to the point where I could float by myself. What concerned him was the possibility of my accidentally falling into water and drowning. He figured that if I could float on my own, I'd be able to hold on until help arrived. This was why he felt the need for special training in the pool.

I Floated!

At the next session, I made it in. At first I just got wet with Sensei holding me in his arms. This wasn't so bad. Next came putting my face in the water. I was okay as long as it only covered my mouth, but I panicked when it came up over my nose. Somehow, though, with Sensei's assistance, I got to the point where I could duck under the surface. Now it was time to float.

With his hands supporting me, I lay on my back. My limbs tensed and my body curled up tight. When he talked me into extending my arms and legs, although his hands were still under me, I had the sensation of floating. But that was as far as I got. Every time he asked, "Can I let go now?" the answer was an emphatic "No!"

Once, though, while I was practicing lying on my stomach on the surface and putting my face in the water, he snuck his hands away for an instant. It was barely a fraction of a second, but there was no doubt about it: I'd floated.

"Ototake, you did it!"

Sensei ran me through this again and again, gradually lengthening the time he let go. One second became two, two seconds became three. Eventually I was able to stay afloat for over ten seconds. But when I turned my head to breathe, I lost my balance and rolled right over. The problem was how to get beyond this point.

I never did succeed in breathing without flipping over, no matter how I worked at it. So, we decided the way to go was for me to propel myself forward until I ran out of air. But the question was how, since I couldn't paddle with my arms.

All I could do was flutter my legs, which are slightly longer than my arms. I fluttered them like crazy, but this didn't work too well either. Since they're different lengths, the more I kicked the further I veered off course. On a bad day, I went round and round in circles on the spot.

Six meters. That was the distance I could swim after five years' work. And then came the summer of sixth grade.

A Craft Project

For the distance swimming meet, students had to complete the full twenty-five meters, no matter what. The other children who couldn't swim the whole length of the pool were able to make it by putting their feet down once or twice on the way. But I couldn't touch the bottom. And so my goal for the year became to complete the lap using a flotation device. The first one I tried was a string of floats tied around my waist, but this was a flop because my head sank while my hips stayed on the surface. Next I tackled a kickboard, but this was no good either. As soon as I climbed on, it submerged completely. It didn't have enough buoyancy to support my weight.

Then, just when we were stumped, we came across some interesting information. We heard of a humongous polyurethane mat, nearly four foot square, called a "floating island." Maybe this would be able to hold me up.

Oka Sensei went straight out and bought one. It was a whopper, all right, and took up a lot of space in the classroom. We carried it down to the poolside for an impromptu craft project.

Sensei handled the carving tools—a paper cutter and kitchen knife—while his junior assistants followed his directions.

Sensei: "Now, Masahiro, you hold that end."

Masahiro: "Sensei, we've got to make it look really good, right?"

First, the front end was pared down to a streamlined shape to reduce resistance in the water. Next, the back end was shaped to my body. Since I moved forward by thrashing from the hips down, I'd be lying on the mat from my stomach up. It took a number of fittings to get it right.

Sensei: "Okay, Susumu, let's put Hiro on board and try it out."

Taking off his T-shirt, Susumu splashed into the water. He placed me on the mat and gave it a nudge from behind.

Susumu: "It's still no good. It'll only sink again, 'cos his weight is resting too far forward."

After many more adjustments, it was just about ready when there was a setback.

Minoru: "Sensei, Oto can't stay on with no hands, the mat's too smooth."

All: "Oh!"

And so Oka Sensei punched in two round holes, one on the right and one on the left. They were exactly like a pair of eyes, making the mat look like a human face. Then he told me to stick my arms through. It worked: with my arms inserted in the holes, there was no risk of being separated from the mat.

That was how my partner for the summer was born. We christened it the "Super Kickboard."

Those Ladies Are Crying

September 9, the day of the distance swimming meet, finally arrived. As the event was held jointly by three local primary schools, the kids from the other schools would be watching too. I was fired up: I'd have to make it look good.

When the boys' twenty-five meters freestyle was announced, my adrenaline level started rising. It was time to show the results of all the training I'd put in with my partner—though, admittedly, even if it *was* called a freestyle event, swimming with a homemade kickboard was unheard-of. Then suddenly the last group was summoned. I was on.

"Group 19. In Lane 1, Hirotada Ototake, Yohga Elementary."

There's an extra big cheer, which is kind of embarrassing. As I mount the starting block, I feel my heart racing. At the crisp *crack!* of the starting pistol I plunge in headfirst. Anybody watching for the first time might think I'd toppled in by mistake, but this is the "dive" I've been perfecting all summer.

When I surface, I paddle once, twice. Then Minoru and Susumu, who are waiting in the pool, scoop me up onto the Super Kickboard and send me on my way with a good shove. The long voyage has begun.

As always, I keep up a steady pace until about halfway. But the water is cold. My legs won't do what I want. The others plow ahead and are gone, and I'm alone in the large pool. You could hear a pin drop.

But all at once the silence is shattered by rousing cheers and applause—and it's coming from the other two schools. It's as if they'd been dumbstruck at the sight of me diving off the block and piloting my kickboard, and have only just snapped out of it. I'm happy to have the other schools rooting for me, but it's kind of a weird feeling.

When I finally finish the length, it has taken me nearly two minutes. Even so, there's a renewed round of applause from the other schools. It's what you might call an ovation, and it goes on and on.

Meanwhile, one of the boys in my class is reporting to Oka Sensei: "See over there, Sensei? Those ladies are crying!" He has a puzzled look in his eyes, as if it's a very strange sight.

Sensei recalls that this made him happier than anything else that day. He said to himself: These children see Ototake simply as a classmate. As far as they're concerned, the fact that he finished the twenty-five meters is not a big deal—the way they see it, one of them just did the same thing that they've all done.

And so Sensei found himself fighting back his own impulse to hug me and say, "That was quite a feat for someone in your condition." Instead, he yelled, "One minute fifty-seven seconds? You never take that long!"

But these words carried an unspoken message that came from the heart: "Congratulations. You've got yourself some real pals who don't see you as special."

Disabled People to the Rescue

A Burden? A Drag?

During the six years I spent at Yohga Elementary, with many people supporting and watching over me, I gained more than I can say. I'm very glad that I was able to attend a mainstream school.

I don't deny the value of special schools. Depending on the degree and nature of their disabilities, some children may need special education. But the important thing to consider is what each individual child really needs.

Back when I started school, it was automatically assumed that children with disabilities would go to special schools, or be placed in special classes within mainstream schools. The stereotype was that they just couldn't cope with the regular routines and coursework. This is simply not true.

True, when a person with a disability plunges right into the general community, in this case by entering a regular school, there are sure to be many things he or she can't do alone, and times when other people are put to extra trouble. But remember how, at elementary school, the kids who

77

caught on quickly helped the slower ones with their lessons, and the kids who could do a backward somersault on the high bar taught the ones who couldn't? Well, that same attitude is all it takes. If there's a child in the class who doesn't have the use of his legs, all it takes is for someone to push his wheelchair. If there's a hearing-impaired child in the class, then it's enough if her neighbor shares his notes. That's all it takes for the people who are grouped together as "the disabled" to receive a regular education too.

But even today, when the parents of a child with a disability want him to attend a mainstream school, they are strongly advised against it. "Since there are special schools available for children like your son," they're asked, "why don't you apply there?" One reason for this response is a fear of criticism from other parents—above all, fear of the complaint that their children will suffer because a child with a disability will take up too much of the teacher's time.

Is there any truth to this idea that a disabled child is a burden and a drag on the rest of the class?

The True-or-False Game

In the fourth grade, we performed a gymnastic routine using sticks for Sports Day. It was a dance done in pairs. In previous years, my partner on occasions like this had always been Takagi Sensei.

That year, however, some of the fourth graders said, "We'll be Oto-chan's partners." Of course, my pair would go at a slower pace and would have to skip some parts. Since my partner would have to hold back, Sensei says at first he wasn't so sure it was a good idea. But because the children themselves had volunteered, he decided to leave it up to us.

Four days after Sports Day, at a parents' association meeting, I'm told the mother of my partner for the performance had this to say: "Thank you very much for pairing my son with Ototake. I just can't tell you how thrilled I was when they danced together and when he got to push the wheelchair in the final parade. Our son is very lucky." She came back to the subject a number of times.

Sensei was caught off balance: having half expected to be taken to task, he never imagined he'd be thanked. It seems the other parents were watching over me with all the warmth that this mother's words suggest.

When our teachers visited the other students' homes, I'm told I was often mentioned. "It's certainly a plus for the others to have Ototake in the class," a parent would say. "And we can't help bringing him up as an example—you know, 'Look at how hard Ototake tries in spite of his handicaps. I wish you'd try as hard.'"

Once, when Takagi Sensei was away, the teacher from next door took us for PE. Told to bring one ball per person from the storeroom, several children came back carrying one in each hand. When she scolded them, they answered, "I brought one for Ototake."

After seeing them take turns playing catch with me, she reported to Takagi Sensei, "The children in Room 1 are all really sweet, aren't they?" I'm sure he beamed with pride.

At a reunion of my sixth-grade class a couple of years ago, Oka Sensei told me, "Thanks to your being with us, Hiro, this turned into a wonderfully thoughtful class where it was natural for everyone to help each other out when they were in trouble."

He may have said this out of his own typical thoughtfulness, so that I wouldn't feel inferior, but something tells me it wasn't completely off base. A friend who teaches nursery school once remarked, "Since this spring, I've had a child with Down's syndrome in my class. At first, as you'd expect, the children were frightened and kept their distance, but within a month or two the whole class began to develop a spirit of kindness, and it all revolved around the child with Down's."

I hear stories like this all the time. Just about every class that has a disabled child in it seems to turn out remarkably well.

At Yohga Elementary, the effects weren't confined to one classroom, either. The month I started school, preparations were under way for the annual party to welcome new students, and the sixth graders in charge of the planning were reporting their decisions to the staff.

"For the party game this year, we've decided on True-or-False. If you think something's true, you nod. If you think it's false, you shake your head. The subjects will be—"

"Hold on a minute," a teacher interrupted, thinking of the usual scramble to separate into "true" and "false" camps on opposite sides of the playground. "How will you tell who gets the answers right, with hundreds of people just nodding?"

"But, Sensei. This year there's Ototake. He can't take

part unless we do it like this." The way the student said this, as if it were obvious, made the teachers look at one another, momentarily lost for words.

In today's competitive society where one is always expected to excel, we're losing sight of what's obvious—when you see someone having trouble, you lend a hand. We've been hearing for a long time now about the breakdown of communities whose members used to help one another. It could be that the people who come to the rescue, the people who can rebuild a more fully human society, will be people with disabilities.

2

Full Speed Ahead

*My Middle School, High School,
and Cram School Years*

The Dribbler!?

What the . . . !!

The transition to middle school was my smoothest. There was something reassuring about going to Yohga Junior High, the local public school, with my old classmates from Yohga Elementary. The school officials basically had no objections, and I was able to enroll with no trouble. I guess it counted in my favor that I'd been attending elementary school without an escort since third grade and obviously enjoying life at school as much as anyone, if not more.

The great thing about middle school life is the after-school clubs, which go into high gear during these three years. Guess which one I belonged to? It may be a bit of a stretch. No arms, no legs, in a power wheelchair: a kid with disabilities like this would most likely head home at the end of the day and read a book. Or if he joined a group, it would probably tend to be one of the more sedentary ones. Well, this kid signed up for—basketball!

Was I out of my mind? My motive was very simple. By the time they reach junior or senior high, people start to go in different directions: the energetic, high-spirited kids to the sports clubs, the serious, quiet types to the cultural clubs. Most of my friends were full of energy and high spirits (judging by the amount of trouble they got into) and almost all of them had signed up for a sports club, so I thought "I will too." I wanted to join; I joined. In the process, the possibility that it might be too much for me, or a nuisance to everyone else, completely slipped my one-track mind.

This magnitude 7.8 earthquake struck the Ototake household first. It took a lot to shock my parents, who were accustomed by now to their problem child's bizarre behavior, but this time even they were stunned.

Father: "What the . . . !!"

Mother: "I just don't understand how our son's mind operates."

When I was born, my parents had decided on a policy for my education: they would bring me up to be strong. Whatever else they did, they wouldn't raise a child who ran away from things, using his disability as an excuse. But this time, I'm told, they wondered if they hadn't gone too far.

The problem child was not to be talked out of it, however. Not knowing where to turn, they phoned the vice principal.

Mother: "Uh, my son has just come home and calmly told us he's joined the basketball club . . . "

Vice Principal: "Yes, well, I've discussed it with the coach, and since it's what the young man says he wants to do . . . "

Mother: "I do hope it won't inconvenience the other students . . . "

Vice Principal: "Well, it's not as if he'll be playing in games . . . "

Coach

Shrreee! The referee's whistle shrills. "Substitution, Yohga, No. 8."

The other team and the crowd all turn and look at the Yohga bench. But no one gets up. They see only the coach's confident smile. Then, glancing down, they spot a player hauling his butt out onto the court. Yes!!

Any coach who would play me had to be as nuts as I was. Ours was an original, to put it mildly. He was a ton of fun. A big bear of a man with a shaved head, a beard, and a heavy, rolling gait. If you gazed out the window during class and saw a figure striking a sort of tai chi pose for no apparent reason, that'd be Coach. This unconventional teacher was, in short, Yohga Junior High's celebrated "character."

He wasn't just eccentric, though. Nothing ever fazed him. He took everything in stride; that was his style. Perhaps the school allowed me to sign up for basketball because the club had such a big-hearted coach.

Going back, then, to when I joined up. So far so good, but—you've got to be wondering—how on earth did I play? I couldn't lob the ball high enough to shoot baskets, but I could make passes over a fair distance, thanks to the workout that my shoulder muscles had gotten playing dodgeball in elementary school. But it took more than that to get me off the bench. I had a selling point, and that was dribbling.

Not in a wheelchair, as you might imagine (especially since there's a whole sport called wheelchair basketball). I got down and moved around under my own power. I was already confident of my quickness—I could turn on a dime. Now I just had to combine these moves with ball handling. In other words, how much of my speed and mobility could I keep up while dribbling the ball? That was the question.

First, I practiced until I could keep up my rhythm. *Dumdumdumdumdumdum.* It wasn't easy. Other people bounce a ball just below waist height, which means they have a split second before it comes back. Since I dribble a ball at around the height of most people's calves, however, it hits the ground and returns in no time, so I have to keep my arms moving on the double. This was the hardest part.

Next came dribbling while in motion. This wasn't too easy either. The ball had ideas of its own. I was always bumping it against my legs or sending it rolling every which way. Little by little, though, I began to see results, and before I knew it I could dribble almost as fast as I could run.

One look is worth a hundred words, as the Japanese proverb says. No matter how much explaining I do, it's probably quite hard to picture. It's too bad I can't put on a demonstration for you!

Drills, Drills, Drills

My teammates were surprised by my progress, but since they'd known me from grade school they'd probably had an idea that I could manage this much. It was the coach who got a real surprise. When I said I wanted to join the basketball club, no doubt he'd figured I would just be getting some exercise. But from here on in, his reaction was terrific.

Coach: "Ototake, you've gotten very good. I'm amazed. Now how about practicing dribbling with your right arm as well as your left?"

Ototake: "But I've only just gotten the hang of it on the left, and I'm left-handed. I've never tried it on the right, and—"

Coach: "So, that's what practicing is for."

Duh! It was my claim to fame that I'd try anything once, and Coach had beaten me at my own game. Back to square one. First, I practiced just bouncing the ball. Since I don't use my right arm much, I was already in trouble—I couldn't seem to keep it straight. When I finally had that down, it was time for dribbling on the move. But I couldn't get the hang of it on the right side. The ball did what it wanted, my movements were clumsy. Improvement came more slowly than in the left-handed drills.

After working with the ball day in and day out, I gradually got used to handling it on the right. Now I could dribble on either side. I was so high on my own progress, I couldn't wait to show Coach. But when I triumphantly showed off my right-handed dribble, his reaction was unexpected.

Coach: "Nice work, Ototake. The next step is to try a crossover. You want to practice switching the ball to the other side quickly."

Ototake: " . . . ???"

Coach: "When a defender comes from the right, you dribble on the left. When he's on your left, you dribble on the right. If you can switch fast, you won't give it up easily."

Defender? What defender? Whoa—is he talking about a game? If I do this assignment well, Coach is planning to play me.

I trained intensely. Switch left-to-right. Switch right-to-left. A quick turn of the shoulder. Keep the speed up as you switch. I also worked on a spin move to fake out that "defender." Dribbling right-handed was still the hang-up, though. I kept losing the ball on the crossover. The monotonous drills were sometimes a drag, but I never wanted to quit.

One thing kept me going: I wanted to find out what it was like to play in a game. Thinking about it now, I realize I may have been deluding myself. Maybe Coach had no thought of playing me; maybe he was just giving me something new to do so I wouldn't get bored. It would be kind of funny if he'd ended up having to play me because I was so darn fired up about a game.

Secret Weapon

Whatever the real story might have been, once I was in, I was partying. Playing in a game felt just as good as I'd expected. If you've shot a few hoops, you'll know that the lower your dribble, the harder it is to steal. Mine is bound to be below the other players' knees. I call it the subterranean dribble.

We must have boggled the other teams' minds. While they're still wondering, "Can this guy *walk*?" he starts dribbling, then slips past below knee level, slices through (under?) the wall of dithering defenders and drives down the court with his nifty dribble. That was my job.

Our captain was a great three-point shooter. He would get open and in close enough for me to complete a pass. Then he'd turn and sink a three-pointer. Another great assist by the self-styled "secret weapon."

But even though I called myself the secret weapon, if a halfway decent team seriously came after the ball they could take it away with no trouble, and our defense was really loose. Let's face it, we might as well have been playing four-on-five. Coach, of course, has my heartfelt gratitude for giving me the chance to play regardless—and so do my teammates. In fact, when I said I wanted to join the club, they were the ones who persuaded him by offering to keep an eye on me.

I was a pest during practices, too. As I worked on drills in a corner of the gym, the ball was forever rolling out onto the court and interrupting play. And anybody could see that our team's strength would be reduced if I took the court. But no one ever showed the slightest resentment. They always called out, "Let's go, Oto. Relax, we're with you, man." As younger students entered the club, they must have wanted the chance to play themselves, but they swallowed their feelings and cheered me on with all their might. Some of them even accompanied me to and from away games.

I owe my happy memories of club time to the cooperation of everyone who let me have my own crazy way. I'm proud to think that my being on the roster was a symbol of great teamwork.

When I open my graduation album, there I am, wearing

the No. 8 jersey and a big grin. I got that smile as a present from the whole team.

The Festival Guy

One-on-One

I'm often called "the festival guy." It's true, I love festivals.
I used to go to all the fairs at the neighborhood shrine, and
my heart beats faster at the sound of flutes and drums.

I've always loved not just actual festivals but any festive
occasion. Partying under the cherry blossoms, birthdays,
class outings, fireworks displays, school plays, Christmas,
New Year's . . . Whenever I heard of an upcoming event,
whether in or out of school, I always felt a buzz of excitement.

In middle school, the two big annual events are Sports
Day and the Cultural Festival. At Sports Days, although I'd
get into the spirit, my body wouldn't follow through. For a
disabled person, to play a major role at Sports Day is only
a dream (though when it comes to being cheered on and
applauded by the parents, I may have been a star). And so
I set my sights on the Cultural Festival. I wanted to get
involved, put it together, and, above all, have fun.

You couldn't just volunteer for the job, though. Each
class elected one boy and one girl to the Cultural Committee,

which did the work for the festival, arranged parties for the graduating students and the incoming freshmen, and so on. There was also a Cultural Steering Committee which coordinated all these events; one boy and one girl were elected to this from each grade. I decided to run for the Steering Committee in the second semester of seventh grade.

My rival was the guy who lived across the street—the same one who'd proposed the Terrible Trio's cleanup after the shrine fair. He was a pretty tough opponent, talented in sports and academics, an outstanding leader who headed up the Sports Day cheering squad. We'd had a friendly rivalry going in class committee elections since grade school. As far as liking the spotlight was concerned, we were evenly matched. The time had come for a showdown.

It was close: only a dozen votes separated us. He could easily have won. I still remember that day—how I waited for the results after class, almost praying. He was doing the same. The count came in. I was happy at winning, but my feelings were mixed. We had fought fair and square, but somehow I felt bad for him.

Being neighbors, we naturally went home the same way. He took me by surprise by saying, "I'm comin' over to hang out at your place."

That made me feel better. I remember even more clearly what happened when we got home. "I lost to Oto," he told my mother. "By a few votes. Bummer."

"And you still came home with him? Boys are so uncomplicated."

No, you don't get it, I wanted to say. It's not because boys are uncomplicated. He was thinking of my feelings, even though it meant swallowing his own disappointment at such a near miss. I wonder what he's doing now? He used to dream of going to med school. I hope he has. I know he'd make a good doctor.

The Candidate

Being on the committee was even more fun than I'd imagined: making and putting up posters after school, getting to know the older students, who seemed very grown-up, and the teachers—once, when we stayed especially late, the vice principal had ramen noodles delivered for us all.

Gradually, though, I wanted to do more. The Steering Committee only got involved once a program was finalized. That wasn't enough for me. The real decision-making body was the five-member Student Council: the President, the Vice President, and the chairs of the Cultural, Sports, and Campus Steering Committees. After I'd been working on the Cultural Steering Committee for a while, I started aspiring to be its chair.

When the Student Council elections came around in December of my eighth-grade year, of course I ran for the position. But at this point an unexpected rival appeared. A boy from the Swimming Club. He'd never been the type who took part in committees and things until now. It was rumored that he was running because he wanted the extra points that Student Council members get on their transcripts.

I caught fire. I didn't know whether that rumor was true, but I prided myself on having served three straight terms on the CSC. You wouldn't catch me losing to a guy who was running for the sake of his student record.

Even in junior high, we were required to make election speeches. We had to make the rounds of the classrooms during lunch breaks. Facing the senior classes was the worst hurdle—I was really nervous at the prospect.

Then a powerful backer appeared: Waka-san, the senior who was the current chair of the CSC. We had been on the committee together for a year and a half, and he was especially kind to me. He was captain of the baseball team, a very outgoing personality, admired by everyone. When he offered to go around with me and make a campaign speech, it gave me a real boost.

After I spoke, Waka-san would take over and talk about my work on the committee. He was hugely popular among the seniors. I'm sure he was much more effective than I would have been if I'd spoken for my whole five minutes.

I also called on the cooperation of some seventh graders. I asked the CSC reps, basketball club members, and students I knew by sight from my neighborhood to stir things up when I came to their classrooms.

"Yo! Ototake-san!!" Rousing yells filled the air as I entered. Guys, I thought, you're going too far. But they sure did stir things up. The seventh graders who didn't know much about me must have gotten the impression that I was pretty popular.

My grueling (?!) campaign was rewarded by a landslide victory. There were three candidates for CSC chair, but I drew almost two-thirds of the vote. Thanks, of course, to Waka-san and the seventh graders.

Boy, that junior high school wasn't afraid of anything. First it lets a guy in a wheelchair into the basketball club; then it elects him to the Student Council.

Empty Cans and Ghost Stories

On January 4, the five newly elected Student Council members got together. We made a New Year's visit to Meiji Shrine to pray for the success of the council's future activities. Someone had suggested that we'd get into the mood better if we went on the first day of the year, but because of my wheelchair the other members chose to wait until the massive crowds that gather on the first three days of January had dwindled. We were a team. I prayed: "Please let me work to create a great festival with this wonderful group."

Besides the festival, we planned all the school events, from Sports Day on. Since we also gave the opening and closing speeches at each event, I had an increasing number of opportunities to speak in front of people.

Another major job was marshaling the whole school for morning assembly. "Quiet, please. Each class please form two straight lines." Little did I know, back when I was always too busy chatting to get into line, that one day I'd find myself giving the orders.

These were things that the Student Council routinely did, but we also tried out some new ideas. First, there was the "Good Morning Campaign" that we launched in April. We came half an hour early, waited at the school gates, and said "Good morning" to the students as they arrived. It was a busybody attempt to cheer up those students who started the day walking with their hands thrust into their pockets and their heads down.

Next, we tried recycling cans. The aim was to clean up the streets and raise funds at the same time. We soon found we were onto a good thing—we hadn't realized how many people tossed their cans away. Once we had a few, we childishly wanted more, more, more. We approached liquor stores in the Yohga area: "Excuse me, we're collecting empty cans for our school. Would you mind if we came a couple of times a week and picked up the cans left in the trash containers beside your vending machines?"

While all the owners said okay, they asked us to come just before closing time. And so collecting became a nighttime job: eight or nine o'clock, not the usual hour for a middle school Student Council to meet. But it was fun to explore the city together after dark.

One day on our rounds, the chairman of the Sports Steering Committee said, "Hey, that was a good haul today—let's all go to the park!" We headed for the wide open spaces of nearby Kinuta Park. It was pitch-dark and quite creepy. Just when you were wondering "Where's so-and-so?" —"Gotcha!"—you'd jump out of your skin. Later, we told ghost stories around a flashlight that someone had brought. What started out as a recycling drive had somehow turned into a night of playing Who's the Chicken?

It was after midnight when I got home. Some of the kids caught it from their parents, but today it's a good memory. Maybe the five of us, supposedly the pride of Yohga Junior High, were just a bunch of goof-offs?!

The NEW Cultural Festival

By the autumn of ninth grade, I'd gotten used to working on the Student Council; now it was time for my last Cultural Festival. The usual festival had two parts: an interclass choral competition and an exhibition of works made in art, shop, and home ec classes. The students always practiced extra hard and stayed late to finish their exhibits.

We came up with an idea. Instead of a festival where everybody did their thing and then it was over, we wanted to plan something extra just for the fun of it. We had the perfect excuse: commemorating the opening of the new gym. "A fun festival. A festival to remember." That was our slogan.

It was hard enough preparing the usual kind of festival. But because we already had two years' experience and had seen how the older students went about it, we were pretty sure we knew the procedure. This time, though, there was a new twist, and we were on our own. The headaches began at the planning stage. Even in setting the schedule for making decisions and getting things ready, we were feeling our way.

At the same time, we had fun. Because it was the first time for everyone, we had a real sense of putting something together ourselves. Even simple decisions, such as what music to play as people came into the hall, were batted around and around.

"We need a tune that will liven things up. What about 'Can You Fight Twenty-Four Hours a Day?' " (a vitamin tonic jingle that was a big hit at the time).

"What we need is a classic in a quiet mood. Billy Joel's 'Honesty' would be just right."

By now we'd retired from club activities, and after school we would head straight for the Student Council room at the end of the first-floor corridor and put our heads together over the program.

The main attraction was decided: party games in which the classes would compete. After all that practicing for the choral contest, each class would be tighter than at any other time of the year. Providing a chance for them to go up against each other should generate a lot of excitement—a festival to remember.

The teachers weren't happy at first, but in the end they gave us a free hand. Maybe it was a reward for all the enthusiasm we'd shown so far.

After the regular program was over, all the students gathered in the gym. Representatives of each class came up on stage and competed to see, for example, who could stick their face in a basin of water the longest. The older teachers were clearly not very pleased.

But the audience loved it. It would have been a waste to let that hyped-up mood just fade away after the official program was over. We'd looked for some way to keep it going, and we hit the jackpot. We hadn't expected such screaming excitement ourselves.

Perhaps it wasn't exactly what you'd call "cultural." But we achieved what we'd set out to do and gave the students what they wanted, and by those standards it was a very satisfying Cultural Festival.

What good is an event, after all, if it isn't fun? That's why they call me "the festival guy."

Yatchan

Reserved Seats

Young people are said to grow wildest during the junior high school years. They have a lot on their minds: personal relationships, their academic future, love. A vague anxiety constantly sets their nerves on edge. Their parents only tell them to study, their teachers do nothing but tie them down with rules. Their frustration builds up. And then, in the timeless way, it's turned on those weaker than themselves. Junior high is the stage at which bullying is most common.

What happens when a disabled person, who is seen as a weaker member of society, enters such an environment? This was the main concern those around me had when I started junior high. They were afraid that my friends might no longer be so friendly. We would all be growing up. They might not spend time with me as they used to, they might not help me any more. I have to admit to feeling a little uneasy myself.

To add to these concerns, nearly half the students at Yohga Junior High came from another neighboring elementary school. I would have to make new friends. There's a big difference between making friends when you're six or seven and when you're twelve or thirteen and have reached the age of reason. My disability, which in first grade had been an asset in making friends, would now be a burden. I wasn't sure I could carry this off . . .

To go back to the beginning of seventh grade: when our homeroom classes were announced, sure enough, I was surrounded by unfamiliar faces. I looked around the classroom for someone I might begin to make friends with. In the midst of all the commotion, there was one boy slumped at his desk with a bored look. This was my first encounter with Yatchan.

We'd gone to the same elementary school, but were never in the same class and had hardly ever talked. He was a quick thinker and certainly not bad at his studies in those days. He was also athletic, one of the five best swimmers in Setagaya Ward. In sixth grade, he was a leader in his class.

In junior high, though, he gradually changed. Everything seemed to be too much trouble, and little by little he began to cut classes. He hardly ever spoke to his classmates. You could see a pack of cigarettes more or less concealed in his jacket pocket. He was the type the teachers called "delinquent."

I was intrigued by him. He seemed to have a certain quality that I lacked. Tall and handsome, he was popular with the girls. Even a boy could see how cool he was. His way of looking at things out of the corner of his eye gave him an aura all his own. Next to the other new junior high students—really only glorified sixth graders—he seemed very mature.

There was a place at school—the landing of the stairs —that was his reserved seat. He was always sitting there lost in thought. Sometimes alone, sometimes with his pals. One recess, I happened to look up the stairway. As usual, he was there. He was on his own. I seemed to remember he'd left class during the last period saying he didn't feel well, and had supposedly gone to the infirmary.

I'd been thinking all along I'd like to make friends with him, but there hadn't been any real opportunity. Before I knew it, I was on my way up the stairs. My heart thudded faster with each step, as if I was about to ask a girl for a date. I perched next to him, my heart racing. He glanced over but didn't seem to take much notice. Whew. I'd been secretly afraid he would snarl, "This is my place. Get lost."

I don't remember what we talked about; maybe we hardly talked at all. I only remember an indescribable sense of being at ease I'd never felt before. I was so comfortable there that soon I had a reserved seat of my own.

A Lonely Leader

He may have been what was called a "bad kid," but he certainly wasn't bad at heart. He took no part in the widespread bullying, and he didn't start fights.

Part of his appeal must have been the way he looked out for others. Once, before a particularly unpopular teacher arrived in class, one of the boys stamped a blackboard eraser all over the teacher's desk, covering it with chalk dust. The boy did it to rile him, and it worked. The matter was reported to our homeroom teacher, and suspicion at once fell on Yatchan.

The teachers all eyed him accusingly. We heard he was given a grilling by our homeroom teacher. Yatchan would never have pulled such a childish prank, but, to our astonishment, he took the rap.

"Why don't you tell them the truth?" It may have been the first time I'd spoken sharply to him. "We all saw who did it."

"I don't mind, Oto. I'm their usual suspect anyway. It'd be mean to go and rat on the other guy."

What could I say? While admiring him all the more for his sense of honor, I felt sad that Yatchan had given up on himself.

People sought his company. Boys with pent-up emotions they couldn't handle on their own. He didn't give them advice or help, but they came anyway. It was enough just to hang out with him, I guess. Maybe there was something healing about it. And maybe I was one of them.

He looked lonesome, though. Surrounded by all those companions he was, for some reason, alone. That solitary air of his made me feel lonely myself—I wanted to understand him and earn his trust.

There was trouble, once, when one of his buddies got into a fight and made some threats using his name. Yatchan's status as "the boss" at Yohga Junior High meant that his fame had spread to other schools, and the kid who'd gotten into a tight spot may have thought he could get out of it by using his name.

Yatchan didn't like fights, as I've said. But since his

friends turned to him whenever they had problems among themselves, he was constantly caught up in feuds. And so his reputation traveled ahead of him. Now it was happening again. He hadn't wanted to cause trouble, but he was dragged into a quarrel with another school.

After the incident, he seemed even more alone—at least, that was how it looked to me. For a while, he distanced himself from his usual companions. Perhaps he was sick of dealing with that scene and all its hassles.

He seemed comfortable around me, since I wasn't involved in the incident; in fact, I didn't even know the whole story. The two of us spent more time together. During recess, we were always in our reserved seats. And not only during recess—gradually we began going there during class time as well. I thought this wasn't right, of course, but I told myself it was only temporary.

I knew he'd go back to his crowd again. Whether he liked it or not, they wouldn't forget Yatchan, the head honcho of Yohga Junior High. They couldn't get by without him, and he wasn't the kind of guy who would let them down. He was simply taking time out. He was probably just weary; he wanted a break from his usual world, and he'd chosen me to keep him company.

On fine days, we skipped class and hung around in a nearby park.

"Want one, Oto?" he'd say, exhaling a lazy cloud of cigarette smoke.

"No, not for me."

"Uh-huh."

He never insisted. I wasn't completely guilt-free about

cutting classes, but whatever guilt I felt was blown away by my happiness at being with him.

My Guardian Angel

The teachers weren't too thrilled. Though they distrusted Yatchan, they apparently didn't jump to the conclusion that he was bullying me. But they did think he was exerting a bad influence on me. I was told, "Don't get too mixed up with him," and the same was spelled out to Yatchan too. The teachers seemed to have the wrong idea about him.

Going back to where I began: What happens when a disabled person, who is perceived as weak, enters the emotionally turbulent world of middle school? Most likely he will be bullied. Especially if he's as pushy as I was at the time. I'd joined the basketball club, I was on a committee. I stood out in my year. In other words, I was the kind of "smart aleck" that some people no doubt would have liked to teach a lesson. If the truth be told, there were probably kids who thought, "That guy makes me puke." But I was never bullied.

I think Yatchan's presence must have made a big difference. The other students may have regarded him with a variety of feelings—awe, hero-worship, respect—but all agreed he was definitely someone you didn't take lightly. And there was I, his sidekick. That probably made it difficult to bully me. You could say he was my guardian angel.

It's true he wasn't the type who gets straight A's and listens to the teachers. Okay, so maybe in their eyes he was a "problem student" and a "delinquent." But when I think of all the kids Yatchan rescued—kids who couldn't talk to the teachers about their troubles—I wonder if it's right to slap the label "loser" on a boy who, just by existing, was able to make those troubles go away.

Yatchan came to see me once after we graduated.

"That's great, Oto, you going to a top high school. Me, I dropped out in the end. No diploma here."

He'd left high school and become an electrician. For the job he'd had to get his hair cut, dye it again—black instead of bleached-out brown—and bite the bullet no matter what his customers said. Next to a solid citizen like him I was still a kid.

"But, Yatchan, I'm still sponging off my parents. You're working, you earn your own living. *You're* great."

"Think so? Nah . . . " He flashed the appealing embarrassed grin I hadn't seen in a while.

I wonder whether, nearly ten years later, our reserved seats are still a favorite hangout at the junior high. And whether the kids all have a lot on their minds.

A Love Letter ♥

A Springtime Incident

By the start of ninth grade, I was on the Student Council
and becoming known around the school. As the new students
arrived that April, I began to realize that I was actually in my
final year of middle school. At basketball, too, we were all
practicing hard together for our last tournament. You could
say that life was full in every way.

That spring, there was an Incident.

I think it was during art class. There was a prod from
the boy behind me. "Ototake, a first-year girl said to give you
this."

"What is it?"

"How should I know?" He snickered. Not a . . . ?
I snatched the envelope and, careful not to let the teacher
catch me, opened it up. The handwriting wasn't the cute
round style of most teenage girls. The lines were written in
a clear, flowing style.

Hello. You probably don't know who I am, but I

know you. I see you at the gates every morning,
greeting people with the other members of the
Student Council. I always feel refreshed and ready
to face the day when you say "Good morning."
Lately, though, I've been feeling a little down,
because I have to come early to train for the Inter-
High athletics and I don't get the chance to say
good morning to you, my very favorite ninth grader.
I used to look forward to that every morning and I
really miss it. I promise I'll do my best at training,
though. You keep up the good work too.
NAME, Class 4, Seventh Grade

The chisel I was holding shook so much I nearly cut myself. I realized my face was bright red. People must have wondered what was wrong with me. I tried desperately to look as though nothing had happened, but the corners of my mouth were stretching wider and wider and there was nothing I could do about it. I went drifting off into a daze. Totally out of it.

A love letter. The first I ever received.

A Young Man's Heart

Her letter meant more to me than I understood at the time. I'd always believed that love could grow between me and someone I might get to know in classes or clubs or committees, if we talked and communicated and she came to understand what I was like as a person. That had been my idea of love until then.

But this girl was different. I didn't even know her by sight, let alone to talk to. She couldn't possibly know what I was like. If I call it a plain old crush she might be upset with me, but in fact it was the kind of crush that younger students get on older students all the time. So, okay, we could just say there's no accounting for tastes and let it go at that. But the thing is, she must have liked the look of me, wheelchair and all.

It's not that I wasn't popular with girls. On Valentine's Day I received as many chocolates as any boy in the class, if not more (in Japan, the girls give the boys chocolates on Valentine's Day). But these weren't the special "you're the one" chocolates. It was just that, since I talked with boys and girls alike, I was friendly with many of the girls, and they would bring one gift for the boy they *really* liked plus one for Oto-chan. So when I say I was popular it sounds good, but it doesn't mean I was the type that girls fall in love with.

In elementary school, I'd watch out of the corner of my eye as the girls squealed about how gorgeous the boys on the soccer team were. I was envious, but I knew I wasn't the heartthrob type. I knew a guy in a wheelchair couldn't hope to catch the girls' eyes just by the way he looked—to attract their interest, I mean, not their curiosity or sympathy. I felt that way, I have to admit, but at the same time I told myself that a disability had nothing to do with love. Mine was a complicated young man's heart.

These tangled feelings became still more painful when I reached middle school. As we entered adolescence, romances were blossoming. Of course, it was the good-looking guys who were popular with the girls. Although I tried to fake it by telling myself that looks aren't important, it's what's inside that counts, I still didn't see any girls beating down my door. As I continued to be just a friend who was fun to talk with, I can't deny thinking that even I would have a chance if only I had arms and legs.

Barriers to Love

A single letter blew all this away. We'd never talked, and yet she sensed something in me. It was like being told that, all along, I'd been okay just the way I was. I was on top of the world. I don't mean I thought I was God's gift to women, but simply that I began to have confidence in myself and in the possibility of love. "Hey, how about that?" I thought. "I can have an ordinary relationship too."

I'm not saying that a disability is never an issue when it comes to love. It happens: a boy gives a girl the brush-off because he just can't see himself going with a girl in a wheelchair; a girl dumps a boy by telling him, "I can't communicate with you because of your hearing problem." No matter how brave a face we may put on it, the hard fact is that people with disabilities do have a handicap in love.

But I think the important thing is not to turn your disability into an excuse. True, when your heart's just been broken, it may be the first thing you think of. If only I could see, if only I could hear . . . But was that the real reason it didn't work out? Even the most beautiful woman in the world may be unlucky in love. Love never goes exactly as you want. And besides, who'd be attracted in the first place to somebody who's so down on themselves? "I'm disabled, so what can I expect? Women only feel sorry for me. I don't stand a chance." That's a pretty effective way of driving away the love you might have found.

Some men prefer tall women, some women go for chubby guys. My mother declares, "Handsome men make me uncomfortable." (My father, of course, asks with a wry laugh, "So what does that make me?") I don't suppose a disability is actually an asset in too many people's eyes, but don't let that stop you. In the end, it all comes down to what you, as a person, have to offer.

If you said to a girl something like, "Sure, I'm disabled. But I've got better taste in clothes *and* more brains than that other guy. And, believe me, nobody could care for you more than I do," your chances of getting her attention would go up significantly. (Though it may sound a bit corny.)

I received several more notes from the girl who wrote to me, and souvenirs from places she'd been. In the end, I wasn't able to return her feelings. But it was she who gave me a whole lot more courage when it comes to love.

I wonder if she still has the second button from my school blazer (the one the girls like to ask the boys for at graduation because it's nearest the heart)?

Exam Capers

Choosing a High School

In their third year of junior high, everyone begins to grow
restless. Some kids comb the high school listings looking
for entrance requirements that match their level on practice tests, others shriek over the best-looking outfits in the
uniform catalogs. Everybody takes to carrying around exam
guides. It's a heady time of mingled hope and anxiety.

Like everyone else, I was agonizing over choosing a
school. It was not that I didn't have somewhere in mind.
Toyama Metropolitan High—a school with a tradition that
goes back over a hundred years.

The orthopedic surgeon who'd treated me since I was
little had often talked about Toyama High. A keen sports fan,
he had taken on the job of team doctor for their American
Football Club.

"You don't often see such fine young men these days.
Their dedication to football is impressive. They've got character, too, and above all they've got guts."

When I started thinking about where I wanted to go, I

immediately remembered these words. I wanted to meet these great guys, and maybe end up becoming a fine young man myself.

Dream on. To get from Yohga to Takadanobaba, where Toyama High is located, would take nearly an hour by train and involve changing lines. Traveling by train in a wheelchair is difficult enough, but commuting every morning in those unbelievable rush hour crowds was all but impossible.

I would have to give up. Or so it seemed, until my father made a startling suggestion.

"We can move."

"Wha . . . ?????"

"Let's move within wheelchair commuting distance of Toyama High."

"But . . . "

"No problem. My office is in Shinjuku anyway. It'll be more convenient for me."

We'd moved to Yohga in the first place because it was handier to my kindergarten. Even to contemplate the effort and expense (as much as six months' rent up front) all over again . . .

For a while I thought over whether or not to take up my parents' generous offer. No, it was way too much to ask. But then again, if it was a question of finding a high school I wanted to go to within reach of our house in Yohga, the answer was that there wasn't one.

And so I decided to take advantage of their bold and extraordinarily thoughtful proposal. To live up to their generosity, I started studying in earnest. This would have been around June.

Thrills

At an interview with my parents present, I was told by my homeroom teacher that I was aiming too high. Toyama was the hardest of the metropolitan schools to get into. "You have only a fifty-fifty chance of being admitted, and even then, there's no guarantee you'll be able to keep up once you're in."

I'd been warned. No doubt he was right. But I didn't care—I still wanted to go to Toyama High. That was the one thought in my head.

But there were adverse circumstances. Under the admission system of the metropolitan high schools, you can't count on getting in simply by doing well on the day of the exams, because more weight is given to your school reports. The higher your grades, the lower the score you have to get on the exams, and vice versa.

Nearly everyone who tried for Toyama High had straight A's. That meant that on the entrance exams they had to get a minimum of 420, which averages out to 84 per subject. Unless something went very wrong on exam day, they were home free. But in my case, although my grades weren't bad in the five exam subjects (English, Japanese, math, social studies, and science), there was a catch: phys ed.

Since middle schools rate your performance relative to your peers, I inevitably scored low in phys ed. This naturally dragged down my total, so that the minimum I had to get on exam day shot up to 460, or 92 per subject. It wasn't going to be easy.

For once, I was really in a cold sweat. Since I was only trying for the one school, I had to pass, no matter what. I had visions of spending a year cramming at home as a junior-high *rōnin*, a "masterless samurai," waiting to have another crack at getting into my school of choice. It was an alarming thought.

Thrill City

Six months went by in a flash, and the exam season was upon us. And then my parents did something so rash it sent chills down my spine.

We were going to have to move for me to go to Toyama. Our choice of apartments was quite limited, because not many places check out when you have all the constraints that arise with using a wheelchair—no steps at the entrance to the building, an elevator if we lived above the first floor, room to park the chair in the (usually tiny) hallway, and so on. Add the fact that we had to be able to move in precisely at the beginning of April, and our options were practically zero.

Miraculously, one apartment turned up. But, we were told, there was someone else interested who was still wavering. It was up for grabs, so to speak—and so, would you believe it, my parents go and sign the lease!

I was stunned. It was definitely the right move if I passed, but the key word was *if.* Looking back, I don't know whether to praise their decisiveness or be amazed at their recklessness.

Even more shocking was the fact that they told me. Normal parents, even if they signed the lease, would surely have kept quiet about it so as not to increase the pressure on their son. But not my folks.

"We've already signed the lease, so you'll have to pass, or we're in trouble." It's a rare parent who piles on the pressure like this.

"But I don't know if I can . . . "

"Well, do your best."

Okay, okay, I get the point, but still . . . What was it they said when I signed up for basketball? "I just don't understand how our son's mind operates." I wanted to say the same thing to them. But perhaps I was wrong to expect them to behave like normal parents—for it was clear to me now how I'd come by my own reckless nature.

A Rainy Day in March

I've always been good at not blowing it on the big day—never fluffed my lines in the drama festival, never choked at the crucial moment. So I could be confident of that much. This time, however, the bar was set too high. My chances really were fifty-fifty.

The pass list was due to be posted a week after the exams, on March 3, Dolls Festival Day. Of course, I was planning to go and look at the bulletin board myself, but it rained that day. We decided my mother would go and look.

The results were to be released at 10:00 A.M. When my mother's call still hadn't come by half past, I couldn't help thinking . . . Trying to put such ominous thoughts out of my head, I told myself there must be a long line at the pay phone. This was before the days of cell phones, and there was no way for me to contact her. Was she wondering how to console me? I learned then what it means for time to stand still.

It was nearly eleven when the phone rang: I'd passed. It turned out that my mother had fallen into the clutches of a famously talkative acquaintance on the way there. Why today, of all days? God plays some pretty mean tricks.

It didn't seem real at first, maybe because I hadn't seen the notice for myself; all the same, happiness welled up slowly inside me. I was vaguely thinking, "So hard work does pay off." And we wouldn't have to break the lease. In retrospect, my parents say they signed because they had faith in me, but even with all the faith in the world, that took some nerve. Still, it turns out they're only human. They told me later that in the month before the entrance exams, they could barely eat for anxiety. I felt a little guilty when I heard this, but then, judging by the fact that I didn't notice a thing at the time, I guess I wasn't too calm myself.

Anyhow, I'd passed. The whole song and dance certainly hadn't been easy. But all my worries evaporated the moment I heard the good news. What began to occupy my mind instead was the new life that would start in a month's time and the new encounters that awaited me. What did the next three years have in store?

Twenty-Five Warriors

Turned to Stone

In April 1992, I became a freshman at Toyama Metropolitan High School. We newcomers were given the red-carpet treatment by the upperclassmen.

Toyama has a lively student activities scene, and there were over forty clubs scrambling for new members. Before classes and during breaks, squads of athletes in their team uniforms ran whooping down the hallways, while the performing arts groups came charging into our classrooms and struck up a tune or staged an impromptu skit. Basically, we freshmen were overwhelmed by all the enthusiasm.

I was getting on well with a kid named Ryo. At 6′ 2″ and 198 pounds, you couldn't miss him in a crowd. Naturally, the sports clubs were all over him; his desk was always surrounded by recruiters at recess.

We sat near each other and, it's true, I envied all the fuss being made over Ryo right before my eyes. Not that I wasn't getting invitations too, of course: the *go* and *shogi* (Japanese chess) clubs, the chorus, the literary society . . .

but none of those interested me.

It must have been about four days into the semester. Once again, the upperclassmen from the sports clubs were right there in front of me, swarming around Ryo's desk. I made up my mind to speak to one of them.

"Uh, I'd like to join too . . . "

When the recruiter looked around and saw who was speaking, he froze as if turned to stone. And no wonder: I'd picked the one who was suited up in gladiator gear and carrying a helmet in his hand. Yup, he was from the American Football Club. Looking him in the eye, I asked again: "Please let me join the Football Club."

As for what I could do once I joined, I hadn't given that a thought. My orthopedist's words about the gutsy guys on the football team—which were what made me want to go to Toyama in the first place—just naturally seemed to lead me in this direction. I was joining because I wanted to: it was that simple. Like the time I signed up for basketball, the word "disability" never crossed my mind.

My Spot on the Team

Football being more of a contact sport than basketball, I wouldn't be seeing action as a player. I signed on as a manager, but out of all the usual duties—such as getting drinks ready, taping ankles, and buying supplies at sports goods stores—there wasn't a single one that I could do. Feeling pretty impatient with myself, I let off steam at practices by yelling twice as loud as anyone else. Could I really be useful to the team, or would I only be a drag? I didn't know, but I just wanted to zap thoughts like that right out of my head.

The coaches saw at once what was going on with me. They thought hard about whether there was anything I could do, and what they came up with was a job at the computer. This would be my first return to the keyboard since the end of sixth grade, three years earlier.

In Japan, at least, American football has the image of a sport where big men slam into each other. And that's true enough, as far as it goes. Even at the high school level, linemen weigh in at over two hundred pounds, and when you see them, padded and helmeted, rushing their opponents, it may look more like a martial art than a field sport. But there's more to the game than meets the eye. In fact, together with its human cannonball aspect, it has an important mental component—strategy, in other words. American football is played half with the body, half with the mind.

The job I was given was keeping stats: collecting data on the teams we faced and entering them in the computer, then analyzing them for strategic use in the next game. "In a case like this, x percent of Team A's plays are to the right side, y percent to the left. In this situation, they pass x percent and run y percent of the time." It was my task to tabulate these statistics for the coaches. Before a big game, I would often pull an all-nighter gathering data from a stack of videos.

That wasn't my only job. I was also allowed to sit in on the coaches' meetings when they decided the freshmen's positions, and to give directions during practices. I was no expert, but there are points that someone watching from the sidelines can see more clearly than the players themselves.

So I was neither a player nor a manager. My duties were something like a coach's, but I wasn't exactly a coach, either. My role was very loosely defined. Because it was so free-floating, though, the coaching staff actually expected all the more of me, seeing me as an important conduit between the players, managers, and coaches. And I was able to find my spot on the team at last.

How 'bout Those Hornets?

Our team—the Toyama Green Hornets—was pretty strong, though when it comes to sheer physical size, we weren't even in the same league as the private high schools. As a metro-politan school whose admissions were based almost entirely on academics, we had to include boys in the ninety-pound class just to scrape together enough players, while some of the private schools' clubs could even hold tryouts, they had so many star athletes to choose from. Judged by size alone, we would probably have been one of the five worst teams in Tokyo.

But what we lacked in terms of muscle, we more than made up for with leadership. Our coaching staff, headed by two former All-Japan players, must have been among the finest in the country. Thanks to their solid tutoring in strat-egy and mental preparation, the Green Hornets had become a high-powered team that always made it to the Tokyo dis-trict semifinals.

Somewhere along the line, our rallying cry had become "Kanto Champions." To beat players twice our size and be the No. 1 team in the Kanto (East Japan) region: that was our dream. By the spring of my eleventh-grade year, we were on the way to making that dream a reality.

In the quarterfinals for the Tokyo district title, we found ourselves facing the top contender, Nichidai High School No. 3. True to its name, the Black Resistance, their team wore black from head to toe. Just the sight of them was enough to strike terror into their opponents.

They were in fact a formidable team. At Nichidai H.S. No. 3, players built like Ryo were a dime a dozen. And they weren't just big, they were strong and fast. Our players said, "They're like a huge wall moving with lightning speed right before your eyes." That was what we were up against.

But it was a must-win game. Only four teams from Tokyo would go on to the Kanto championship, which meant we had to reach the semifinals, and that meant beating Nichidai. If we lost, it was the end of the road. The seniors were due to retire. It was an all-or-nothing situation.

The showdown took place in the rain—football truly is an all-weather sport. We weren't in bad shape, but the Resistance bolted ahead and set the pace. As a steady drizzle fell, a grim mood settled over our bench. But not one of us gave up hope.

In the fourth quarter, the clock was ticking against us. Our squad put up a last-ditch battle. You could no longer make out the Hornets' colors of green and yellow through the mud on their uniforms. You could barely see the numbers on their backs, and yet our men shone as they fought toward their dream.

For my part, all I could do was yell. And tell our guys what a great job they were doing as they came back to the bench during the changeovers. I never felt powerless, though, because, like them, I had something important to do: believe in my teammates and victory.

14–12. A come-from-behind win with seconds to spare. We had each played our part to the end, never losing hope, and that was what clinched it. I couldn't stop shaking. Then, on the verge of tears, I saw a startling scene. A senior who never showed his emotions—he was famous for it—was on his knees on the turf, crying like a baby. I couldn't hold back my own tears as what we'd done, and how glad I was to be on this team, really hit me.

Their faces smeared with mud, rain, sweat, and tears, my teammates formed a circle and thrust their helmets high into the air with a roar that sent a chill down my spine. That day, they—no, *we* knew why football was our game.

After our dramatic comeback against Nichidai, we were on a roll. We went on to win the Tokyo pennant for the second time in Toyama's history.

But the final curtain fell all too quickly. In the first round of the Kanto Regionals we played the Shizuoka Prefecture champions, Mishima High. The game went back and forth, and when the clock ran out the score stood at 28–28. Under tournament rules, the winner would be decided by a toss-up. As we watched on the sideline, the referee flipped a coin and, moments later, our captain hunched over with his head in his hands. Our dream had slipped away.

For two years, from tenth grade until our last games during the spring tournament of senior year, we'd been football-crazy. Our minds were constantly on the game—in the street, during class, in the bath. It had meant everything to us at high school. With football gone from our lives, each of us felt a crushing emptiness.

It didn't take us long, though, to realize what mattered the most: in setting out together to capture the Kanto trophy, we had each found twenty-four comrades we could be proud of.

Water of Life

Michio

The Toyama Festival is held every September. As a rule, the tenth graders put on art and science displays, the eleventh graders perform plays, and each senior class makes a movie. This program stands a little bit apart from the kind of festival that's currently popular at other schools. For parents and friends who attend, the usual parties and food stalls might be more fun than having to watch amateur plays and movies. But for us, on the production side, Toyama's kind of festival was the best you could have.

Our senior class had already made a start on its movie project the previous fall, in eleventh grade. We began by choosing the director. The kids I'd gotten friendly with working on our play that year told me I was the only possible choice, and they'd back me up. Since I've always liked getting attention and taking charge, I thought this wasn't a bad idea at all. Egged on by the others, I could really see myself as the director. But it turned out not to be so simple.

There was another boy, Michio, planning to try for the

job. He belonged to the football club, and we'd been friends since tenth grade. As a running back, he was nicknamed "mojo man" because he had the exceptional body control and balance we associated with African-American players. He tanned really dark, too—at summer training camp, after lights-out, all you could see of him were his white teeth and white T-shirt standing out in the night.

His athletic brilliance wasn't the only thing about him that attracted people. He also had a kind of charisma that's difficult to describe. I'd always known I was no match for Michio.

I never felt outdone by kids who slaved away at their books. Of course, this wasn't because I was confident of doing better than them in school; I just didn't measure people by their grades. Then what was it about Michio that had me beat? In a word, it was his big heart. He seemed to have a kind of bottomless capacity for life. A free spirit that was never hung up about anything. Next to him, I was made aware of my own smallness as a human being.

When Michio went for director, I was disappointed, yet at the same time I was glad. I thought, "There goes my chance," but I was also full of high hopes for the film we could make with him in charge. I never felt for a moment that it should be me instead. He seemed exactly the right person for the top job.

Several classmates who didn't know his true worth kept pushing for me. But instead of going along, I talked them out of it. "If you want a really good movie," I argued, "Michio's your man, not me."

And so the project got under way with Michio as director and me as assistant director.

Life

It took us nearly six months to decide our theme and complete the script. Once, we rejected a script that was almost finalized after two or three months' work. Starting over took a lot of courage. But people said, "Hey, if we're going to make a movie, let's make one we can all feel good about." And we headed back to the drawing board.

It was already May by the time work started on the final script, once we'd officially decided our theme. The theme was "death." Or perhaps "staying alive" would be more like it. You can tell what a hot topic this was among high school students at the time from the fact that, at that year's National High School Drama Festival, most of the sixteen schools in the final selection did plays on the theme of "death."

This was our plot. Sixteen-year-old Toru and his mother live alone. Several years ago, his older sister committed suicide and his father died in a drunken fight. Since then, life has lost its meaning for Toru. But as he becomes aware of his mother's love for his father, for his sister, and for himself, he gradually realizes that he must going on living. One day, Minami, the girl he's deeply in love with, is taken to the hospital after an accident. Toru is devastated. His father, who he thought was dead, appears to tell him how precious life is and how important human beings are

—every single one of them. But it's only a dream. When Toru wakes up, he learns that Minami has regained consciousness, and rushes to her side. Seeing her again, he realizes something that he had lost sight of: how good it is just to be alive.

We weren't pros; it was the work of high school students. Maybe it sounds cheap and hokey, but I was happy, because the story got our message across in a way that anyone could understand. In fact, when one of my classmates produced this script, my reaction was "Why didn't I think of that?!" I was amazed that a kid my own age had thought about these things and could write about them so well. If any readers are interested, try the drama section of your nearest video store where you'll find it . . . not!

Michio, who read a lot and had a broad general knowledge, gave the movie its title. He chose *Usquebaugh*. This Gaelic word (the root of "whiskey") means "water of life." He said he'd been struck by the way the word takes something we use every day without thinking—water—and puts it together with "life." Perhaps that's a sign of how greatly water was once valued in Europe.

So, what was it that we valued? Michio explained that he'd chosen this title in order to pose just that question: what was precious to each one of us?

Having received the name *Usquebaugh*, our movie, too, began to come to life.

Different Flavors

Filming began in earnest in mid-July, after first-term finals, and lasted about a month. But things didn't go too smoothly, because we had the heat to contend with. Mid-July through mid-August is the hottest time of the year in Japan, and filming all day under a blazing sun was a real ordeal. I got off lightly, though, compared to the cast. They had to perform to our strict director's satisfaction with the temperature in the nineties. Some of the kids even had to wear coats for a winter scene. It was hell just to watch them.

But it was the camera, sound, and lighting crews who suffered the most. While the rest of us were sweltering just moving ourselves from place to place, they had heavy equipment to lug around. And conditions got worse during the actual shooting—even if sweat ran into their eyes or they were eaten by mosquitoes, they couldn't make a sound, and the cameramen couldn't move a muscle. It took real grit to hold down those jobs.

Eno was the ideal chief cameraman. Voted "Most Likely to Make a Good Father" by the class, he was the strong but gentle type, and he always got jobs done quietly and dependably. When no one else was interested in making the props for our eleventh-grade play, he'd taken them on and constructed a cherry tree practically on his own. Though he liked to stay behind the scenes, we all knew that Eno was the one in our class who saw that things got done.

The combination of Michio and me also worked really well. Each day, my job as assistant director was over before the cameras rolled. I kept track of all the details: where we'd be shooting, what time we'd meet, which members of the cast and crew were needed, where the equipment was, who would take it to the new location, etc., etc.

Then, once the ingredients had been prepared, Michio was the chef. While we were filming he was in complete control. He had the skills and the instincts. Watching him direct, I was glad it wasn't me. I think that, between us, we made the most of what each of us brought to the movie.

Usquebaugh had a subtitle: *One Drop of Water.* It came from the dream scene, where Toru's father tells his son, "A human being is like a drop of water. One drop of water is so tiny that if it fell into the ocean, you'd never know it was there. But the ocean is made up of drops of water, and humanity is like that too. Toru, I get the feeling you're thinking, 'What difference would one less person make?' But this world is made up of people, one by one. Think of it. Each life is worth something. Each life is precious."

I liked those lines. After we'd finished filming, though, I realized the crucial difference between people and water: one drop of water is the same as the next, but people are all different.

This project made me really understand the phrase "the right person in the right job" for the first time. Of course we needed someone like Michio who could direct, but we also needed someone like me who was good at setting things up. And we needed someone like Eno working quietly behind the scenes just as much as we needed the people whose best qualities came out on the screen.

Making the most of what each of us had—our differences—was what enabled us to make a fine movie. For me, it was worth having done the whole project just to learn that.

In the publicity pamphlet for the film, I wrote: "What message do you want to pass on to the next generation? Life is precious, people need each other . . . There are many possibilities, but when you think about them you might notice something you never saw before—the one thing that's most important to you."

Math: 7/200 . . .

A Celebrity!?

Studying was never really my thing. Even after we divided into humanities and science tracks in senior high, I was especially weak in the "easy" math and physics courses that we humanities students took. I knew I wasn't good at science subjects, and that knowledge was faithfully reflected in my grades.

I did reasonably well in the first term tests. Even in math, to my relief, I was about average. But then my scores went rapidly downhill. And no wonder. It would've been strange if they hadn't, the way I ate, slept, and breathed football.

For the honor of the club, though, I have to tell you that some of the members gave everything they had to football and still managed to buckle down and get good grades. But I just couldn't do that. When I throw myself into something, I lose sight of everything else. I'm just not the "all-around" type. And so, for the first time, I started to flunk out.

One day, wheeling down the hallway with a friend from

the club who was quite an underachiever himself, I overheard two girls from the class next door talking in whispers.

A: "Here come the two bozos from the football club."

B: "I heard they got five points between them on the last math test."

A: "You're kidding? *Really*? What a laugh."

I was indignant. To set the record straight, I was about to say, "I'll have you know those five points were all mine. He got zip." But I changed my mind. It would've been the pot calling the kettle black.

This sort of thing happened a lot. I knew I was being laughed at, of course, but it didn't bother me. "Gee," I thought, "people are talking about me. I feel like a celebrity." It was my old love of the limelight again. I didn't feel an ounce of shame. Maybe it takes a real bozo to go that far . . .

My Number Comes Up

Eventually, though, I had to crack the books. My math teacher may have had the patience of a saint, but in the autumn of my tenth-grade year it finally ran out.

She had always taken notice of me, lending me books she liked and so on, and she wasn't the straitlaced type, either—she told us stuff like how she washed her hair with mayonnaise or yogurt ("It's good for the hair and the scalp"). But now she warned me in no uncertain terms:

"You're actually not weak in math at all, you know. It's just that you're so addicted to your club. Unless you get at least forty on the next test, I'll have you suspended from football."

This was serious. How could I think of studying when I was giving my heart and soul to football? Only now football itself was on the line, and I had to make that score of forty percent. This was not so simple, however. It was no use studying just the material that would be in the test, since I didn't have the basics. I read the text over and over, turning back now and then to work out the earlier problems. If you're good at math it might not sound like a big deal, but for me it was hell. I was ready to quit any number of times.

When their backs are to the wall, though, I guess people outdo themselves. Sixty-five percent: a high mark for me, slightly above the class average. It was enough to persuade the teacher to let me stay in the club. After that close call, I enjoyed football all the more—thanks to my weakness in math!

There was a sequel to this story. In eleventh grade I had somebody else for math and didn't see much of the teacher in question. Just before summer vacation, when finals were over, I spotted her on the other side of the street near the school. She seemed to have noticed me, too. Cupping her hands to form a megaphone, she hollered across the wide street: "Ototake, how was the makeup test?"

Sensei, puh-*leez*. Not so loud! And not when I'm with a girl I like a lot—talk about bad timing. And anyway, I didn't *need* a makeup test this time.

I never did get any better at math. In senior year, on top of the five regular exams, there were also a bunch of "scholastic ability tests" to help us choose a college. I took them because I had to, griping all the while, "Why don't they make these things optional?" My performance in the other subjects was nothing to be proud of, but math was a disaster area. I couldn't figure out the questions, never mind the answers, and I gave it up for lost.

Tests always have a way of coming back just when you've forgotten all about them. Oh well, let's see how I did: I checked my paper, but my score wasn't on it. There was only my ID number from the class roll, "7," penciled in the corner.

I looked all over the paper, then peered over the shoulder of the kid in front. Hers had "147" on it. In pencil. Uh-oh . . . I took a peek at my neighbor's. "123." Pencil again. I'd made a big mistake. That "7" wasn't my ID number, it was my score.

Seven out of 200. I never did like math.

Ambitions ⚾

When I Grow Up . . .

"Takagi Sensei, you're our enemy!" I would have been in about second grade when I startled Sensei with this declaration of war.

"Why am I your enemy?"

"Because you're a Yomiuri Giants fan, that's why. Tsutchan and me are Hanshin fans."

"But your father's a Giants fan, isn't he? Is he your enemy too?"

"Yes, he is! So Papa and you should be friends."

"But the Hanshin team's been doing pretty badly, now, hasn't it?"

"Mm. So when I grow up, I'm gonna be a pro and play for Hanshin."

That was the first thing I wanted to be. A pro baseball player: yeah, right. But like other kids who want to be an airline pilot one day and a train conductor the next, my heart wasn't all that set on it. Let me run through the career list that followed.

In third or fourth grade, I announced that I was going to be a professional *shogi* player. Takagi Sensei had taught me to play Japanese chess because he wanted me to have one thing where I could hold my own, and in this intellectual game which tests your ability to think ahead, a disability makes no difference. I was fascinated. I read up on the game and invited friends over to play.

Sensei had expected me to make a good bit of progress in a year or two, but I let him down in a big way. I did get to be one of the better players in the class, but I was no match for him, of course, and more importantly there were also several kids who could beat me every time. By fifth grade I finally realized, "If this is the best I can do, I'll never be a pro."

So, moving right along, in sixth grade I came out with "I want to be President of the United States." I still don't know what gave me that idea. I abandoned it three days later, however, when I heard that in order to be President I'd have to become an American citizen. I really wasn't willing to stop being Japanese. But I didn't think, "If I can't be President of the United States, then I'll be Prime Minister of Japan." Evidently being Prime Minister didn't strike me at the time as a very sexy occupation.

Law?

It was in middle school that I began to have a serious ambition. My chosen profession was law. It started with a small thing: I was being a rebellious teenager, and my mother said sarcastically, "If you're so fond of arguing and talking people

down, why don't you become a lawyer?" I must have forgotten to be rebellious and taken her little dig perfectly
seriously.

"A lawyer . . . Hmmm."

This one conversation set me off on wanting to be a
lawyer for five whole years, but then, in my high school
senior year, I had another change of direction.

One day, I happened to read a newspaper article about
how difficult it is to pass the National Bar Examination.
There was one piece of data, in particular, that grabbed my
attention: the average age of successful candidates was
29.3 years. When you think that most of them would have
started preparing for the exam in college, that meant it took
them nearly ten years to pass the bar. Having to be up to my
eyeballs in study all that time was a very nasty thought.

"Who cares," said a friend, "if life's a bed of roses afterward?" But suddenly I was doubtful: did I really want to
spend the whole of my twenties, a time when people soak
up experience, doing nothing but study?

It wasn't an easy call. I could see that some things
might only be attainable through years of hard work. I'm
not knocking that kind of life, but I knew I wasn't cut out
for it. I didn't have the staying power.

And so I thought over whether I really wanted to be a
lawyer. I thought about how a spat with my mother first put
the idea into my head, and how I'd dreamed of it all this
time. And I realized that I'd really only been interested in
the image. Lawyers were cool.

I was good at public speaking, I might get through the
exam if it involved a lot of rote memorization, and it looked

like there was plenty of money to be made. But when I realized that these, plus the cool image, were my only reasons for aspiring to be a lawyer, I began to feel apologetic toward people who actually practiced law. Surely they must have better motives—wanting to help victims of injustice, believing passionately that everyone is equal in the eyes of the law. But that wasn't where I was coming from. It would be an insult to the profession to go into it this way. Besides, something told me I'd regret it. When the going got tough, image wouldn't get me far.

What matters in choosing a job, I've since come to think, is having a clear idea of what you want to do in society. If you know that, you'll know where to start looking for a job that enables you to do it. If the right job doesn't present itself, create one. Unless you feel that strongly, you probably won't stick with it, and unless you're that involved with what you do, you probably won't take pride in your occupation. Maybe the world is a harsher place than I think, but I'm not about to do a job when my heart isn't in it.

"Lawyers are cool." I'd really put the cart before the horse with that one.

A Wavering Course

I was a smart aleck back then. One of the things I'd often mouthed off about was the way that many people just drifted with the tide in going to college. Why go at all if they didn't know what they wanted to do? But now I found myself in the same boat. When my ambition to be a lawyer faded, I had no alternative in mind. With nothing left that I wanted to do, college no longer seemed relevant to me. I sent out applications without really thinking. But I couldn't focus on college prep in that state. People were urging me to get a degree because "you never know," but that was the whole problem.

I'd retired from the football club, we'd finished our movie, and I wasn't studying for university entrance exams. I was spinning my wheels. For the first time, I learned how hard life is with no goal. Perhaps what I felt was the letdown that came after being continually on the go, charging toward the Kanto Championship and the Toyama Festival.

The last six months of school were gone before I knew it. By graduation time, nearly all of my friends were making a new departure, whether they'd gotten into the college of their choice or were hustling to find a good cram school. I was left behind, all on my lonesome.

Then a friend told me, "Oto, you're too idealistic. How many people have decided what they want to do at eighteen? Of course, it'd be best if you could go to college to study something you've already chosen, but don't you think it's all right to go there and find out what you want to do?"

That woke me up. Okay, then. College it is.

The Joys of Cram School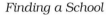

Finding a School

Takadanobaba, where we lived, is a famous student quarter. It's also home to a large number of cram schools for those preparing to take university entrance exams; they attend either in the evenings while they're still in high school, or full-time after they've graduated but failed to get into the college they're aiming for. There are so many cram schools around the station, some famous and some not, that I hardly knew which to choose. Since any one of them would do, as long as it was close to home, I would have thought conditions were ideal. Big mistake.

I dropped by one which I'd heard was very good, according to a friend who went there during senior high.

"Uh, I'd like to come here from next April."

"One moment, please." The receptionist disappeared into the back office. I assumed she'd gone to get me a brochure, but I was dead wrong.

When she returned, she said politely, "The school doesn't have full facilities for wheelchair users, such as elevators and accessible toilets, and so it's not possible for us to accept you."

This came as a bit of a shock, but I shrugged it off and looked elsewhere. Again I was turned down for similar reasons. I tried explaining, "There's no need for an elevator, I can climb the stairs on my own, and I don't mind if there's no wheelchair-accessible toilet." But in the end I was refused on the grounds that "We can't be responsible if anything should happen."

I continued making the rounds without success. At some schools with entrance steps I couldn't even get near enough to ask to be let into the building, and at the worst place I was brushed off with "I'm afraid we can't have people in wheelchairs . . . " Hey, come on, I didn't see any sign outside saying "No Wheelchairs Allowed."

Even so, I wasn't outraged, or heartbroken. Just astonished. "Gosh," I thought, "being in a wheelchair is quite a problem."

Having been lucky enough to grow up with the parents, teachers, and friends that I had, I'd never had any reason to think of myself as "a disabled person." You might even say that this was the first time I'd run up against a brick wall due to my disability.

But this was no time to sit around being astonished. Here I'd made up my mind about college at last and was ready to get to work, and now I couldn't find a place to do it. I really needed a cram school, because I didn't have the willpower to study by myself at home. I was in a jam.

Around this time, I learned from a mailing that came to my address that Sundai Preparatory School, one of the three largest national networks of cram schools, had a branch within reach of my home. Without getting my hopes up too much—surely a major chain would be the least likely of all to take me—I set off at once to check it out. The main building had stairs, but in the new wing there were elevators and no steps. It was fully wheelchair-accessible. Now the only question was whether they would accept me.

The manager who met with me first was reluctant, as I'd expected. "Responsibility" came up. But just as I was about to give up on this school, too, the younger members of the staff urged their boss to reconsider. It must have done some good, because the discussion started moving in a positive direction.

After the interview, I toured the place with one of the younger staff to check out just how accessible it really was.

As we got into the elevator, he said, "Let's give it our best shot together." Those few words cheered me up immensely. The whole ordeal of being refused at every turn was behind me now. I was about to begin my year as a *rōnin*.

The Biker

The school's location, in Okubo, wasn't far from my home by train, but since it's difficult for me to take the train on a daily basis I would have to commute by wheelchair. This took me exactly half an hour. It wasn't convenient, certainly, but considering what a dead end the schools in Takadanobaba had been, I wasn't bothered at all by the extra distance.

Except when it rained. Then I clutched my umbrella

between my left shoulder and my neck, tucking the handle under my leg to steady it in the wind while I drove with my right arm as usual. It was quite a haul. Not only was it an effort to hold that position, but the umbrella blocked my view to the left, making it hard to see traffic lights or cars that came out of nowhere. Traveling for half an hour under these conditions was pretty hairy.

If I hardly ever played hooky, even when it rained, it was because I enjoyed the life. It may sound odd to say that I enjoyed cram school, but I did. It was easy to make friends since we were divided into fixed classes (not classes that changed for each lecture), and, unlike most cram schools, Sundai assigned us fixed seats. Also, the fact that over half the people in my class were trying for the same university may have given us a feeling that we were all in this together.

The first person I got to know was Rikimaru—nearly five foot eleven, long-haired and thin-faced, with looks so sinister that a friend once asked me, "Does he do drugs?" Puffing on a cigarette off by himself during breaks, he struck me as being very unapproachable.

One day, I got back from the drinking fountain to find that class had already started. Outside the door I ran into Rikimaru, who was late back from a cigarette break. We had second thoughts about going in, as the teacher of that particular class was pretty scary, and decided instead to wait it out on a bench downstairs. Rikimaru turned out to be nothing like the image I'd had of him; he was a very friendly, decent guy. We soon hit it off when we discovered that, among other things, an old basketball teammate of mine had been a friend of his at senior high. From then on, we hung out together.

Rikimaru rode a motorbike to school, and was really into bikes. Since I'd never had a biker friend before, there was something about him that seemed new to me. At cram school there were all kinds of students—kids who came from outside Tokyo, kids who'd gone to private schools— and Rikimaru was just one of many people from unfamiliar worlds I got to know. That may have been one reason why I enjoyed myself so much.

Summer vacation is the clincher for cram school students—if you can make yourself work over the break, you stand a chance in the exams. When classes went back at the end of summer, my circle of friends grew rapidly. Although our class was large, at over a hundred students, the atmosphere was more like a regular school than a cram school. A bunch of us had a lot of fun together—taking the morning off and picnicking in Kasai Seaside Park, hitting a restaurant's all-you-can-eat special of the expensive beef dish *shabushabu* and polishing off sixteen platters, staging time trials with my wheelchair in a park at night. In fact, we did more in the fun department than I used to do in my football-crazy high school days. It was around this time that, like most people my age, I got myself a beeper to keep in touch with my friends.

My main occupation for the year, however, was supposed to be studying. Could I really afford to have such a good time . . . ?

A Miracle

Starting Over

I was in a bad way academically, as you'd expect after my high school career. The first class I went to at cram school was English. The teacher kept repeating the letters S, V, O (subject, verb, object), but I didn't have a clue what they stood for. I plucked up the courage to ask the kid next to me.

"Psst. What's this S, V, O? Some sort of code?"

The look he gave me was a cross between indignation and pity—"Is this guy putting me on or could he really be that dumb?"—when in fact I was deadly serious.

Since I hadn't taken practice tests for college entrance in senior high, I had no way of knowing my relative standing, but it was clear that I was more or less bringing up the rear in a class of well over a hundred. I would just have to start from there. How far could I get in a year? I was looking forward to finding that out as if it were somebody else's problem.

Waseda, one of the two most sought-after private universities in the country, was a funny choice for somebody in my position. My image of Waseda was "a happening place." It's often described as a melting pot; to me it seemed a very high-powered, exciting place where individuals with different values could bump up against one another. I had hopes that if I could put myself in their midst, something would happen to me too. You could say I was relying on others to show me the way, and I can't argue with that, but Waseda did seem like the best possible place for someone who was going to college to find out what he wanted to do.

There was another reason, too: it was right there. The apartment where we'd moved so that I could go to Toyama High was five minutes' walk from the main Waseda campus. The School of Literature was directly across the street; you could see it from our window. The School of Science and Engineering was opposite my old school—though with my math there was no need for me to worry about the location of the science buildings. Anyhow, being in the neighborhood gave me a sense of being connected with the place already. If I went somewhere else, we'd have to move again. Waseda was right in front of my eyes. But it was farther than it appeared.

When the first practice tests were returned, I took one look at the results and freaked out. Of the five schools within Waseda I was planning to apply to, my chances of passing had been given the lowest rating, an E, in four cases. The other was a D. I felt as though the result sheet, with its annotation "Need to reconsider," was laughing at me. "What in the world were you thinking? You plan to try for Waseda University with these results?" I'd known in theory that this was about the level of my present ability, and yet, having

147

the facts spelled out to me so clearly was worse than frustrating—it was saddening. Would I ever make it?

Easy Does It

You could say I had my own style of working. People imagine a *rōnin* or cram-school student to be always studying till 2:00 or 3:00 A.M. But that wasn't me. I was in bed by a little after ten nearly every night. You may laugh and say those are a grade-schooler's hours, but it's the truth. With my lack of stamina, when I don't get enough sleep I don't function too well the next day. And so I would crash not long after ten.

Besides, I couldn't study at home. It was partly because I'd slack off, of course, but more important, by the time a bed, closet, and bookshelves were squeezed into my room, there wasn't space for a desk. I could see why friends who came over to our apartment often exclaimed, "Is this really an exam candidate's room?"

Working at home would have meant trying to concentrate in the living room, where my parents watched TV. Instead, I became an early riser. I had breakfast at 6:30 and set out with plenty of time to spare for Sundai's study hall, where I worked until classes started. It was actually a "special" study hall; because the regular one was upstairs in the main building, which had no elevators, a preparation room on the first floor of the new wing was set aside as "Ototake's study hall." This was a real boon. Since I had it all to myself, it was perfect for concentrating, and I made progress. I went back there after classes and got down to work again.

So, from morning till early evening, I hit the books. When I got home I relaxed, often watching a baseball game with my father, and went to bed a little after ten. People laughed and said, "You certainly go at your own pace," but I took that as a compliment. It's important to set your own pace.

I was doing English, Japanese, and Japanese history. I didn't spend too much time on Japanese since I figured that, up to a point, you either had the knack or you didn't. I already had a solid grounding in Japanese history, the one subject I'd done seriously in high school, and I calculated that I could probably be ready in time if I started cramming in the fall. That left English, which counted for more points than the other subjects and was considered the key to improving your scores. But I've already described the sorry state of my English.

And so English became my top priority over summer break. In fact, I studied so hard that summer, I amazed myself. Sometimes I studied and ate a meal at the same time. (Warning to children: Don't try this at home!) I think I must have put in a good ten hours a day.

In the fall I went back to living at my own pace, but the summer's efforts showed spectacular results. From being near the bottom of the class, my grades rose right before my eyes. By September I was in the middle, and by winter I was in the top ten.

All the same, I didn't kid myself that I was almost there. In the practice tests, my chances of getting into Waseda continued to be rated E or D. Now and then I'd think I'd done pretty well, but even so I only managed a C. I was definitely coming along, but apparently I was still falling far short of Waseda's admissions level. I won't say I didn't feel pressed for time, but I kept on at my own pace, telling myself I had several months left.

My Horoscope

January 15. For most people it's a public holiday, Coming-of-Age Day, but for students trying for national universities it's the date of the nationwide "Center Exams." Because I was applying just to Waseda, which is private, I didn't have to take them, but I took a stab at the questions when they were published in the newspaper the next day. Only half seriously, of course.

An hour later, I was wishing I hadn't. I'd heard at cram school that you'd have trouble in Waseda's entrance tests if you scored below ninety on the Center Exams, and I'd gotten seventy in Japanese history, which was supposed to be my best subject. I was too scared even to try the English and Japanese questions. I made a show of reassuring my parents: "Don't worry, don't worry, they say the Center's history questions are quite different from Waseda's." But as I spoke, I could tell the blood had drained from my face.

February 1 marked the start of the entrance exam season for the main private universities. Within a week or two I received several calls from ecstatic friends who'd gotten into one college or another. Since I hadn't even had my exams yet, this only added to my growing jitters. Waseda's were the last on the schedule.

To take my mind off the wait, I worked through some old Waseda entrance exams. When I finished scoring myself, I couldn't help saying out loud, "Huh???" I'd averaged over seventy percent in my three subjects—for Japanese history I'd gotten eighty to ninety percent. Thinking there must be some mistake, I tried several more years' worth, and again I did pretty well. How was this possible? Maybe, just maybe . . . My hopes soared.

On February 20, my exams finally started. Since I was trying for five schools, I faced five straight days of exams. They lasted practically all day long. It would be a strain physically, but I'd just have to rely on willpower if I was going to achieve my cherished goal of gaining admission to Waseda University.

The first day was the School of Education. Because it allocated more points than the other schools to my strongest subject, Japanese history, if I could get into any of them, this would be it. But there was an unforeseen crisis. In the second hour of the history paper, I suddenly needed to go to the bathroom. It was probably due to the unusually cold weather, plus tension. I made it through somehow. There was a break between the second and third hours, but I can't use the bathroom by myself. All I could do was hold on and wait for the third hour to start.

It went from bad to worse, until I could only hold it by rocking in my seat. Just my luck: this hour's paper was Japanese. Unlike history, where you can simply transfer what you've memorized onto the page in front of you, here comprehension and thinking skills count for everything. But my head was so full of wanting to go, there was no room in there for the authors' intentions.

That was that, then. A year's work. Lost because I had to pee.

March 1. The first pass lists were due to go up. They included not only the (ahem) School of Education, but also the School of Political Science and Economics, which was said to have the strictest standards of all Waseda's schools. I knew my chances were slim. I'd scored myself using the model answers that the cram schools had given out a few days earlier, and I was right on the borderline. But nobody believed me at home when I said there was a glimmer of hope. And why should they? One of the schools we were talking about was the one where I couldn't think straight during the exams because I'd had to go; the other was the toughest humanities school to get into at any private university. Maybe I was wrong to hope.

My parents' attitude was a clear contrast to my own upbeat mood. They told me later that they weren't worrying over whether or not I would pass—nooo, they were discussing how to be tactful when I came home crushed. The daily horoscope on TV that morning was the final blow for them. For my sign, Aries, it said, "You will be embarrassed in front of a lot of people." They don't usually believe in horoscopes, but on this occasion, they say, they completely gave up hope.

It was pouring. Praying that I wouldn't be crying in the rain, I headed for the site just five minutes away. I was there before I'd had time to think. Because my mother had ended up going to look on my behalf when I'd taken the high school entrance exams, this was my first experience of scanning the pass lists. I'd pictured myself pushing my way through the crowd to the bulletin boards like a character in a TV drama, and it was a letdown when there weren't enough people there to push through. For those who'd already passed at several other colleges, I guess it wasn't worth coming out first thing in the pouring rain. Thinking "Those other guys haven't got their hearts set on Waseda like I have" or some such nonsense, I turned first to the board of the School of Political Science and Economics.

Reciting 4-6-6-4, 4-6-6-4, 4-6-6-4 under my breath, I ran my eye down the list. Gee, that's funny. I looked twice, three times, four, but there was no mistaking it. For some reason, the digits 4664 were on display. Hmm, could my number have been 6446? I took out my ID to double-check, but sure enough, 4664 was right there in black and white. I'd made it. To Waseda. Me!

I needed somebody to pinch me. How could I have passed? And in all five schools, as it turned out. Since I'd only known that I wanted to go to Waseda, I hadn't thought about *what* to study, or expected to be given a choice. I agonized over it for a week or so.

The entrance ceremony took place a month later. I attended as a freshman in the Department of Political Science, School of Political Science and Economics, Waseda University.

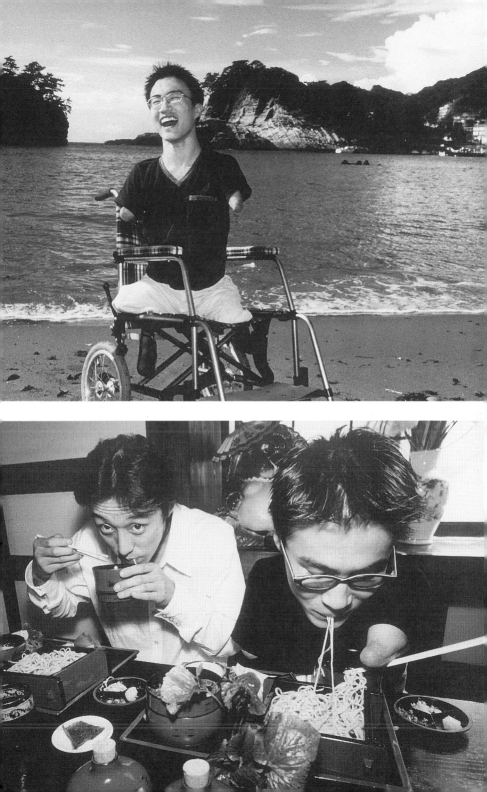

3

The Barrier-Free Heart

My Time at Waseda University

Beginner's Luck

Odd Men Out

The 1996 entrance ceremony was held in drizzling rain. The crowd on campus that day was fantastic. Nearly ten thousand new students assembled, while hordes of returning students champed at the bit to recruit them to club activities.

I should have been fairly used to recruiting drives after the frenzy at Toyama High, but this was something else. A freshman strolling around the campus for thirty minutes or so with both hands held out would end up with a stack of nearly a hundred flyers.

But we were completely out of the loop. By "we" I mean three of my teammates from football days and me. All four of us had become *rōnin* and made it together to Waseda a year later. Perhaps it was only natural to steer clear of us: Ryo, the giant, who stood head and shoulders above the confusion. Nari, our former captain, with his commanding presence and fortyish face. Kage, in his sharp black suit which reminded people a little of the Mafia. And as for me, I had hair down to my shoulders, and even with the best will in the world you couldn't say I looked good in a suit. My friends teased me about it mercilessly.

If I'd been a recruiter and a bunch of dudes like us came along, I probably wouldn't have spoken to us either. After we'd been circulating for a while, Kage suddenly let out a yell.

"What's his problem? Just when I'm finally about to be given a flyer, he looks at my face and takes it back!"

"Can't blame him. Must be those mean eyes of yours."

"Right."

"Oh yeah? Look who's talking."

There wasn't a trace of first-day nerves among us. You could tell at a glance which kids had just arrived alone in Tokyo—they looked forlorn, clutching their registration packets and gazing around. In contrast, we'd been attending schools in the area for four years. It was our backyard. With so many cronies there, besides us four from the football team, it would have been strange if we hadn't felt at home. Whatever the explanation, we definitely had the attitude to go with those hulking frames, and no sign of a freshman's freshness at all.

Together with the old gang, I was starting my life at college. Now to choose a club . . .

"Fourscore and Seven Years Ago"

As I wasn't being rushed by the recruiters, I could only find a club that interested me and make contact. With other freshmen getting the hard sell all around me, it took quite a bit of courage to go up to someone myself and say, "Uh, I'd like more information . . . "

My old teammates would be playing college football. With Toyama's alumni as their mainstay, the Waseda Rebels had become unbeatable in the Kanto region. Our old dream of being Kanto champions seemed likely to come true at last. But the Rebels weren't on my list. Although I'd worked behind the scenes for the high school team for two years, now I wanted to try doing something in my own right. And so I decided that I would root for, but not join, the college football team.

Waseda University is said to have two or three thousand clubs. The one I chose was the English Speaking Society, or E.S.S. I joined partly on a whim, because a friend of mine did, but in the back of my mind there was also the fact that my father, who hardly ever nags, had told me time and again: "Make sure you do English. It'll come in handy."

When I went with my friend to the orientation, I was startled. A lecture theater that seated maybe four hundred was more than half full. According to one of the members, they were a big outfit that welcomed around two hundred new students every year. And it was not only the numbers that took me by surprise. As I was about to find out, the E.S.S. was famous for its demanding program.

On the very first day, I was handed a booklet loaded with English. When I asked what it was, a senior said casually, "Oh, that's the textbook for the speech contest at the end of the month." Uh-oh . . .

The speech contest was a little different from the usual kind: every contestant would be giving exactly the same speech. The men were assigned Lincoln's famous Gettysburg Address. To start with, you had to learn it by heart. From that day on, I found myself turning into a weirdo who went around muttering "of the people, by the people," even on the toilet. Sheesh, and I thought my cramming days were over.

A "Finalist"

Inside, the booklet looked like sheet music: "Put the stress here. Smoothly here. Slow and impassioned here." With everyone giving the same speech, we would be judged on both pronunciation and "interpretation"—power, grandeur, timing, cadence. Since it was a presidential address, one of the main points would be the air of authority with which you delivered the speech.

Well, now, if it was a big attitude they were looking for, I'd say I already had a reputation for that. And—forgetting about my English pronunciation for the moment—I wasn't too bad at speaking in public. I'd been on the middle school Student Council and represented the graduating class at my high school commencement. Stage fright? Never heard of it. So, maybe I should have a crack at becoming one of the—what was that English word—"finalists"?

If two hundred or so freshmen had all presented their speeches one after another, it would have taken all day. And so there was a preliminary round judged by the seniors, from which ten finalists would go on to speak before an audience a week later. If there were a hundred male freshmen, that meant that one in ten would reach the finals. Some of the new members had gone to school overseas. It was going to be pretty intense.

The results of the first round were announced in the club meeting room. As each name was read out there was a stir and scattered applause. They'd gone through eight people and my name hadn't been called. I was just telling myself to forget it when "Ototake" was announced.

The others in my group—we divided into groups for regular meetings—were as excited as if they'd been picked themselves.

"Go for it, Oto."

"We'll be there to cheer you on."

Meanwhile, I was reflecting on the situation. There would be a world of difference between me, who'd gotten myself selected with nothing but a big attitude, and the guys who could really speak English. I just hoped I wouldn't make a spectacle of myself in front of a lot of people.

"Mr. Ototake"

We were told to wear suits for the main event. It was being held in a public hall hired for the occasion, instead of a classroom, and the judges would be native speakers of English. This was more serious than I'd thought. What was I doing on the program? I was really beginning to wonder.

I stepped up my pronunciation practice so as not to make too big a fool of myself. The sound *v*, which doesn't exist in Japanese, is tricky; you have to remember to bite your lower lip. Distinguishing *l* and *r* is difficult too, and as for *th*, I could never get it to sound like anything but a leaking balloon. I certainly wasn't feeling very presidential . . .

I was way down the program, in the afternoon. The finalists in the first half were good, all right—they were really speaking English. When we broke for lunch I couldn't eat a thing. As I muttered away to myself, I couldn't believe how tense I was.

Dammit, if it was a speech in Japanese I'd make short work of the others. Why did it have to be in *English*? My results in high school had never been above average . . . By this time my original goal of improving my English had gotten lost as my old competitiveness reared its head.

"Fourscore and seven years ago . . . " As I began, the hall fell silent. The hush felt indescribably good; I was half intoxicated. Strange what a pleasure it was to speak in front of an audience. When I came to "of the people, by the people, for the people," I felt as though I *was* the President. Call me a loony if you like, but it's true.

"First prize: Mr. Ototake."

I was gazing around, wondering who the winner would be, when every head turned in my direction. It took me a moment to catch on. I had prided myself on holding the audience's attention, but I never dreamed I'd win. When I got home, I stared in a daze at the astonishingly fine trophy.

I'd entered Waseda expecting it to be "a happening place." Maybe more would happen than I'd bargained for. Maybe this was the beginning of something big.

A Waste of Potential 🦋

Vintage '96

Within a couple of months of my dramatic victory, I'd quit
the E.S.S. I originally signed up to keep my friend company,
never intending to stay for four years. But I hadn't meant
to quit so soon either . . . There were two reasons.

First, I'd had enough of the activities. After the speech
contest there was a play in English which we were made to
rehearse out loud in the courtyard. This was embarrassing.
I came up with some excuse or other—"I'm not here to play
games, and I don't remember joining the drama society"—
and skipped rehearsals. The English play definitely speeded
up my exit.

The second reason—the main reason, really—was that
I got busy somewhere else, namely, in the local chapter of a
worldwide student group for international business, AIESEC.
The International Association of Students in Economics and
Business Management (known by its French acronym, pronounced "eye-sek") organizes seminars on career develop-
ment and arranges internship exchanges in many countries.

I've heard it's the largest student organization in the world. This group became my main focus in the first semester, and as the big summer event we were organizing drew near, I got so busy that I dropped out of E.S.S.

AIESEC's members had been preparing for this event, "Vintage '96," for nearly a year. It was on a pretty large scale, costing millions of yen (tens of thousands of dollars). And when you're a student organization, that kind of money doesn't grow on trees, so out we went fund-raising.

The first step was to make a call to a company, outline the project, and ask for an appointment. Often the phone was hung up on us at this stage, but if we could get a hearing we put on our suits, got our business cards ready, and hit the road. If the company showed interest when we'd explained about AIESEC, the purpose of Vintage '96, and its program, we moved on to talk about financial support.

Some folks were critical of us playing at business when we should have been making the most of being students, but this fund-raising work, which was known as "corporate relations," had a big appeal for me.

It's difficult to sum up Vintage '96 in a word. We offered a series of seminars on the theme "life design"—thinking about what to do with your life—with business as the jumping-off point, and invited students from overseas, mainly from other parts of Asia. We rented accommodations at the Olympic Center in Yoyogi for a whole week. During the day, we discussed topics relating to business in each country, went on field trips to observe the current situation in Japan, and so on. At night, we partied. We were students, after all. Big international banquets—or bashes, more like—with food and booze from every country. We got three or four hours' sleep a night.

I had a ball. It's my greatest memory of that summer. But as I continued with AIESEC activities, I realized that I'd gained more than just a great memory. The theme of Vintage '96—life design—had really gotten to me.

By the end of that summer, I was giving serious thought to what I wanted to do with my life.

A Turning Point

One long autumn night when I couldn't sleep, I was thinking things over in an unfocused sort of way. What was I going to do with my life from now on?

That question led directly to "What kind of person do you want to be?" and from there to "What matters most to you?" And I realized something important.

Looking back, I could see that my priorities had always been money and status or prestige. In junior and senior high I'd wanted to be a lawyer, not to help people in need, but because of the cool image and high income. I have to admit, too, that it was the business side of AIESEC that attracted me, rather than its work to promote international understanding. Sad to say, I think I was more interested in making a name for myself in the business world than in understanding other cultures.

But when my own values were brought home to me, I knew that wasn't how I wanted to live. However rich you are, once you're dead it means nothing. And what's the use of status or fame if nobody can stand you? In other words, money and prestige don't necessarily add up to a good life.

What did matter to me, then? That was an easy one. Doing something for other people, for society. Living in a caring way. Understanding and being understood by as many people as possible. All difficult things to do, but I sensed that if I could achieve them I could feel, with pride, that I'd had a happy life. Whatever goals I set myself, though, there was one area where I would never compromise. That bottom line was to value myself.

Then, I wondered, who was this person that I had to value? I wasn't contemplating the Meaning of Life, but I did find myself having to think about who I was.

The first thing that came to mind was three words: "a disabled person." To other people, it may not seem to require a great deal of thought to arrive at this point. But the idea was news to me. Until then, I'd never identified myself as a disabled person.

Up to a point, I could take care of myself. When there was something I simply couldn't do, my parents or friends would lend a hand—quite naturally, not as if they were doing me a favor, just as if they were doing the obvious thing. I'd never been bullied, and I don't remember ever being limited by my disability. I don't mean to give the impression that I'd gotten it into my head that I had arms and legs and was exactly the same as everyone else, but I'd never had any need, or occasion, to see myself as a disabled person.

Once, when I was in fifth grade, a doctor who'd taken care of me since I was little said to my mother, "You know, usually, when a child with limb deficiencies reaches the age of four or five, he becomes aware of being different and asks questions like, 'Why don't I have arms?' or 'Why don't I have legs?' But it didn't happen that way with Hiro, did it?"

My mother says she felt embarrassed, as if the doctor were implying that I was a bit odd. But it's true, I don't remember ever asking those questions or having doubts about myself in that kind of way. I seem to have lived my life not as "a disabled person" but just as "a person," an individual.

In that case, I thought that night, why am I a disabled person? Why was I born with a physical disability in a world where most people are born able-bodied? Surely it must mean something.

While there are things a disabled person can't do, I began to think, there must also be things that *only* a disabled person can do. Take the welfare of people with disabilities, for example. Of course, it's important that politicians and bureaucrats should press for improvements from a policy-making point of view. But a better way to reach people is for an actual wheelchair user like me to point to an actual step and say, "For us, this one step is not just a step, it's a wall." I could give plenty of other examples, but, in any case, it was becoming clear to me that there was definitely something that *only* people with disabilities have it in their power to do. And I began to think maybe I'd been born with this body in order to accomplish whatever that something was.

The next thought that came into my head was, "What the hell am I doing?" If I was born to do something in particular, then I'd been wasting my life. I wasn't making the most of the disability I'd been given. You could say I was letting my potential go to waste.

Merely having a disability wasn't enough; thinking that way would just lead to a misplaced sense of privilege. What was there that I, Hirotada Ototake, with my disability, could do? Taking it a step farther, what was there that *only* Hirotada Ototake could do? If I found the answer to that question and acted on it, I'd have the answer, right there, to what I should do with my life.

By the time I reached this point, it was after 2:00 A.M. But for a while longer I was too excited to sleep. I'd never felt so glad to be alive.

My life had started moving, gathering itself like an ocean swell. November 13, 1996: a night I don't think I'll ever forget.

The Waseda Community Campaign

A Chance Meeting

Once the wave started moving, nothing could stop it. The very next day, in fact, it would sweep me away. The timing was so good it seemed providential.

My late night caught up with me and I overslept a bit. I was on the way to my first class, rubbing the sleep from my eyes, when a voice hailed me. I looked around to see a Mr. Yokouchi, whom I'd met once two months before, standing there. Running into him again like that was quite a coincidence.

Yokouchi-san had given a warm welcome to a group of us from AIESEC when we were drumming up corporate support. He worked at a company called Tokyo Colony—actually it was a nonprofit, but we hadn't done our homework and only discovered that when we got there. They provided printing- and computer-related jobs for people with severe disabilities, who have trouble getting hired by ordinary companies even though they're willing and able to work. Yokouchi-san had taken the time to show us around, and he left a strong impression on me.

And here he was, on the Waseda campus. The circumstances that brought him there were as follows.

Earlier that year, the city government had announced that, starting in December, it would charge businesses a fee to collect their garbage. That put Waseda's local merchants on the spot. They got together and launched a recycling campaign, then organized an event called "Eco-Summer Festival in Waseda."

They found some strong backing for the festival. City Hall promised its full cooperation, and Waseda University loaned them the plaza in front of Okuma Auditorium. The plans grew rapidly. Since it would be embarrassing if an "eco" festival left mountains of litter behind, they set up recycling machines for soda cans and so on, aiming for zero trash on the day. The results were terrific. Although the weather was bad and only 200 cans of beer and soda were sold, 1,300 empties were collected, plus people brought in over 130 of the plastic bottles they normally put out in their burnable garbage. This zero trash effort, which was quite a new idea in Japan, was reported in the national media. The festival had scored a great success on its first attempt.

But a university official scoffed, "What's so successful about zero trash during summer vacation, when nobody's around?" The organizers said to themselves, "Well, if they're going to be like that about it . . . ," and decided to have another try when the campus was crowded with students. And so they were currently working on a "Term-Time Zero Trash Experiment," which would study the volume and composition of the garbage generated in a typical day at Waseda.

And Yokouchi-san, who worked on the campaign in his free time, had come to Waseda that day to help things along.

More Encounters

Yokouchi-san introduced me to the man who was with him: Kitani-san, the head of the local Sanitation Department. He was another supporter of the Waseda campaign, and he told me more about it.

"In the few months we've been working on recycling, we've learned that it's not the only problem the Waseda district is facing. There's disaster prevention, community education, and so on, and they're all connected in complex ways, so we won't get far if we try to solve one problem at a time. Nothing will change unless we move on every front at once. And so we're planning a 'community-building campaign.' One of the things we want to get involved in is what's called the barrier-free movement, to improve accessibility for disabled and elderly people. But that's an area where there's no point in us doing anything unless it reflects the views of the people concerned."

Then Kitani-san said the weirdest thing: "We'd really like your help. How about joining us?"

I couldn't believe my ears. Only the night before, I'd started wanting to live in a way that made the most of my disability, and barely seven hours later I was suddenly being given the chance to do it. What was going on? This was kind of spooky. Although I'm not a believer in any particular religion, it was enough to make me believe in the existence of a higher power.

Before I knew it, I'd answered, "I'll do what I can." But what could I, who'd never even heard the term "barrier-free" before, actually do? I wasn't at all sure, and yet I couldn't let this heaven-sent chance pass me by. The second act of my college life—of my *life*—was beginning.

RENET

The Waseda community group attracted plenty of talent besides the local merchants. Kitani-san and Yokouchi-san were among many people who joined from a variety of backgrounds—government, business, professors, students, the media.

Our mailing list was called "RENET" (short for "Recycle Net"). In my third encounter with computers, I found myself organizing events and exchanging ideas via the Internet. With e-mail, not only could all these very busy people keep in touch around the clock, but whenever we wanted to find out how an issue was dealt with in other countries, members located as far away as London, New York, and Vancouver could send us information in seconds.

The Internet was a more powerful tool than I'd ever imagined. Even though I have a disability, luckily I'm very active, getting out and about all the time. But some people with disabilities like mine can't get out of the house much, for physical and psychological reasons. The computer must be an even more valuable tool for them than it's been for me.

And by making it possible to roam the world while staying in one place, the Web is ushering in a new era for those who are forced to stay at home.

Having connected with the Internet and my new friends, I was ready to go voyaging over a boundless sea.

The Eco-Summer Festival ♪♫

An Echo of RFK

After staging the first Eco-Summer and making a success of Term-Time Zero Trash, the group took the lead in organizing the "Waseda Living Community Campaign."

The simplest way to describe the campaign might be to list its committees. There are six. **Recycling** aims to build a system unique to Waseda, using cutting-edge technology and original ideas. **Barrier-Free** aims to remove barriers from the streets, the university campus, and people's hearts. **Earthquake Preparedness** draws up community-wide plans for disaster prevention, under the slogan "Protect Our Community Ourselves." **Information** works to expand and develop Internet access as the lifeline of our activities. **Community Education** organizes events to foster neighborhood pride and awareness of the issues we're working on. And **Local Enterprise** aims to revitalize local small businesses and the merchants' association, with the focus on "recycling for fun and profit."

The first Eco-Summer Festival had a single theme,

177

recycling. The second time around, each committee put on its own display.

The curtain-raiser was a performance by the Waseda Jitsugyo High School brass band. Then, at the "Eco Forum," we brainstormed about building a better community. In the plaza outside the auditorium, an earthquake simulator on a trailer gave people a taste of "the big one," and the local fire department demonstrated rescue drills. Youngsters excitedly explored an unknown world at the Internet booth, while bargain-hunters thronged the flea market under a blazing sun. In "Wheelchair Rides for Kids," run by Yokouchi-san and myself, children toured the streets of Waseda in a wheelchair and came back rolling their eyes at all the hassles involved.

The grand finale, in the cool of the evening, was an outdoor concert by the Shinjuku Symphony Orchestra. At the planning stage, some people wanted to know what music had to do with the garbage problem, but Yasui-san, the chair of both the merchants' association and the whole campaign, had set his heart on a concert.

When Yasui-san was a boy, Robert Kennedy spoke at Okuma Auditorium during a visit to Japan. This was in the days when protesters were shouting "Down with U.S. imperialism," and as Kennedy left the hall he was surrounded by students chanting "Go home." Young Yasui-san, expecting trouble as he watched from a distance, witnessed a remarkable scene. Taking a mike, Kennedy said he knew a tune, then started singing a song that almost all Japanese know, Waseda University's "Miyako no Seihoku." And, amazingly, the students who'd been heckling him joined in.

Yasui-san remembers getting goose bumps. Music, he says, can rise above ideologies, creeds, and philosophies to bring hearts together. If the young folk listening at the festival felt something of that thrilling sensation, we'd have a better community. That was his hope.

As the Shinjuku Symphony played under the twilight sky, its wonderful harmonies found an echo in people's hearts.

A Proposal

My own involvement in the Eco-Summers began with this second festival. I was given many tasks. Producing advertising flyers for delivery with the daily newspaper to ten thousand homes. Organizing the Wheelchair Rides for Kids, which we did in the hope that by the time those children are grown up and in charge of things, the barriers will be long gone. Making the closing speech at Eco Forum after a hot debate among some distinguished speakers. But my biggest job was presenting a proposal on barrier-free access to the university campus.

Waseda aims to be an "open university," but for people with disabilities there is a high wall to be surmounted. Okuma Auditorium, which is seen as the symbol of the university, is not wheelchair-accessible, and the buildings that have elevators plus accessible toilets can still be counted on the fingers of one hand. The reality is that a comfortable campus life for disabled students is still a long way off.

We decided that during the opening ceremony we

would present the university with a proposal calling for better access. And the job of writing it fell to me, since I was in charge of the barrier-free campaign. (The final text, with some revisions by other members, can be seen on pages 225 –26.)

The proposal was addressed to the President, Dr. Okushima, but as he was away overseas on the actual day, it was presented to the Vice President who attended in his place. I had butterflies with so many people watching, but the ceremony went off well. I got a laugh by telling the audience, "My friends say, 'If the university gets it together, you'll have to go to classes,' " then the Vice President cracked them up with his reply, "We'll give the proposal positive consideration so that Mr. Ototake has no excuse for not coming to class."

This wasn't just lip service—they followed through. The new building completed in the spring of '98 is barrier-free, with full elevator and toilet access, and various other provisions have been made around campus, such as wooden ramps for the steps.

It was certainly rewarding to see our campaign get results in such tangible ways. Now, what to do next?

"He's Okay" 👍

My Favorite Stooge?!

When I got involved in the Waseda campaign, my activities were taken up in the press and on TV; six months later, requests for me to speak, mainly at elementary and middle schools, were coming in from all over the country. I always try my best to schedule in as many of these talks as I can, because I see them as something that only I can do. Until I got used to them, though, I was often unprepared for what happened.

For example: I was sounded out about giving a talk which would fall on the day after my first-term exams. This would be a little hard on me, but the invitation was from a junior college in Shizuoka. And so I talked myself into it, because I had the bright idea that a junior college meant lots of girls. The lecture turned out to be open to the public, however, and the front row was occupied by some very mature "girls."

Having given my talk without a hitch, I was on the point of leaving when one of them rushed over, crying "Sensei!"

181

Thinking she was speaking to the professor who invited me, I turned to look behind me, but nobody was there. She couldn't mean *me*? I was still wondering whether I should answer when she held out an open notebook and asked for my autograph.

I begged off, but it was no use. When she said, "It would be such a thrill if you'd just write your name and the date," what could I do? I wrote, "Hirotada Ototake, July 15, 1997," with the felt-tip pen she handed me, then looked up to ask if that was all right—and froze. There were a dozen people waiting in line behind her!

I suppose what drew them was the sight of me writing with the pen gripped between my arm and my cheek, but—not being a pop star or a celebrity—I never dreamed I'd be holding an autograph session.

When I give talks, it's the contact with children that I enjoy the most. After I've spoken for anywhere between thirty minutes and an hour, I take questions, and the things kids ask always astonish me. Or make me laugh. They have an interesting point of view—kind of unselfconscious.

At one Tokyo primary school, a boy raised his hand: "You're wearing glasses, Ototake-san. How do you take them off?" This was a new one, but I demonstrated, holding them between my arms, then put them on again. There was a stir among the kids, and exclamations of "Wow" and "*Cool.*" While I was wondering how the way someone takes off and puts on his glasses could be cool, another voice from the audience said, "Is he handsome or what?" Aha! So *I* was cool. I was so tickled that, when I joined the kids for lunch, I gave the boy who'd said that my jello. For one so young, he was quite a diplomat.

At a middle school in a Tokyo suburb, there were more questions than I'd allowed time for; I wasn't going to be able to answer them all. The teacher in charge made a move to wrap things up: "We have time for one last question. Who has something they're just dying to ask Ototake-san?"

When I looked around the hall, one boy had his hand up.

The teacher called on him. "Yes, Iwasaki?"

" . . . Um."

"Go on, what's the question you're dying to ask Ototake-san?"

"Which one of the Drifters on TV do you like the best?" (Think "Who's your favorite Stooge?")

The microphone in the teacher's hand was shaking.

Thinking Back

Public speaking is becoming the center of my life. At times I have as many as ten engagements a month. When people say, "It must be hard to squeeze your talks in between classes," I tell them I squeeze my classes in between talks. It's not easy to find the time to go for a stroll, which I love to do, or out with my friends.

When it all gets to be a bit much, as it does sometimes, what keeps me going is something that happened the first time I gave a talk.

In the Living Community Campaign, as we took on a series of environmental projects, we soon realized how important it was to start teaching people about the issues from an early age. And so we ran a program for parents and children, designed to get across the message about recycling, earthquake preparedness, and barrier-free access in a way that kids could easily understand.

Kitani-san and the others wanted me to be the speaker on barrier-free access. I wasn't shy about public speaking as such, but this was a topic I knew nothing about. After all, it was barely a month since I'd first heard the term. And I'd only begun to see myself as a disabled person a month ago. What on earth did they expect me to say?

But Kitani-san wouldn't take no for an answer. "Think of all your experience. That more than makes up for anything you don't know about barrier-free design. You've lived with a disability for over twenty years. Just tell us candidly what it's been like, from your own perspective and in your own words. That'll get through to the children better, I bet."

The program was held in December 1996 at an elementary school gym near Waseda. It was my debut as a lecturer, though I was really just one of several speakers. Deciding that my selling point was being able to see things as a child sees them, I didn't put on a big act, but began to talk in my usual way. I told the kids about day-to-day life using a wheelchair, which I figured they wouldn't know anything about. And I told them that people in wheelchairs were still people just like them, and that each of us is valuable, whether we have a disability or not.

I got a bigger response than I'd expected. Even the parents listened intently.

Our host, Yasui-san, summed up. "Ototake-san said,

'There's something that only I can do.' I hope that each of you young people here today will take these words to heart and think, 'If that's true for him, there must be something that only I can do, too.'"

A month later, I was wheeling home from the university. From the other direction came five or six boys, first or second graders by the look of them, also on their way home from school. When they caught sight of me, they yelled, "What's *that*?" "Gross!" There was nothing new about this— it happens all the time. I didn't take much notice. I was simply letting them go past, when the boy bringing up the rear said something that took me by surprise.

"He's okay."

Eh? I turned and stared. The other boys turned to look at him too, as if to say, "What's gotten into him?" It seemed like he wanted to say more, but he was only in first or second grade. Unable to find the words, he murmured again, "He's okay."

I think he was trying to say something like, "Who cares if that man's riding in a weird machine we've never seen before? He's human, just like us." Frankly, I was amazed. I'm used to being the focus of children's curiosity and hearing them come right out with all kinds of comments. But he was the first who ever reacted like that: "He's okay."

He must have been at the environmental program, I thought. Supposing he was, what if my fifteen-minute talk had touched him somehow and made even a small difference in the way he looks at "the disabled" . . . ?

A couple of words from a boy not yet ten years old have become the source of my campaign work.

Into the Twenty-First Century

Chairperson?!

A week after Eco-Summer, I put on a navy-blue suit and
headed for City Hall. I was going to ask for Shinjuku Ward's
cooperation in a symposium planned for December. I'd first
heard about it several months back when Katsumata-san
of the Waseda Living Community Campaign phoned me.

Katsumata-san himself uses a wheelchair. He's the
managing director of Tokyo Colony, where Yokouchi-san
works, and he also runs a company called Travel Net which
arranges vacations for people with disabilities. He told me
that, three years earlier, he'd helped organize a "Smoother
Travel Symposium" with the theme "Anybody can go anywhere"—the first conference in Japan to focus on tourism
for disabled and elderly people. There'd been a valuable
exchange of ideas among more than three hundred participants, mainly from the travel industry.

Progress had been made in many areas since then,
including an increase in public awareness and improvements in the transport systems. Now, he told me, they were

planning a second symposium, which would take into account the changing social environment and identify issues for the twenty-first century.

Katsumata: "Can we ask you to join us on the committee?"

Ototake: "Me? I don't know if I'd be much help . . . "

Katsumata: "I'm sure you would."

Ototake: "Really? . . . Well, I'd learn a lot myself, so, yes, I would like to take part."

Katsumata: "Good. In that case, I have another favor to ask."

Ototake: "What's that?"

Katsumata: "We'd like you to chair the committee."

Ototake: "Ch-*chair* the committee?!"

A guy barely twenty-one, who didn't know a thing about the first symposium, would have to have *some* nerve to be running the committee. I tried over and over to refuse.

"But," Katsumata-san insisted, "the theme this time is 'Challenges for the Year 2001.' We want to focus on the twenty-first century. That's why we need a talented young man like you for our spokesperson."

Those words, "the twenty-first century," won me over. It was true, I wanted to change society in the twenty-first century—to create a society that was barrier-free.

And so the committee got its clueless chairperson.

Pressure

The symposium's title, "From Barrier-Free Access to Universal

Design 1997," introduced me to another term I'd never heard of. "Universal design" goes a step further than barrier-free access: it's based on the idea that barriers wouldn't have to be removed if they weren't put there in the first place. It means creating spaces that everyone, with or without disabilities, can use. With this "easy access for all" approach, disabled or elderly people don't have to be singled out to have their needs met by special facilities, and therefore don't feel alienated from the rest of the community.

Everything about the symposium, in fact, was a learning experience for me. But knowledge wasn't the only thing I gained. To me, opportunities to meet people are the greatest asset of all, and working on the symposium brought me many new encounters.

One of these was with Mr. Shinozuka. He was the president of a company called SPI which was serving as our secretariat. Originally a tempstaff agency that supplied tour guides, it had branched out into handling travel for elderly and disabled people. I got to know Shinozuka-san through committee meetings, and before long we were having heart-to-heart talks and going drinking together. I got to know his family too, and went grape-picking with them. As I came to trust him, I took the liberty of considering him a kind of older brother I could depend on and look up to.

I learned countless things from him, observing how serious he was about his work, and how he always made time for his family. Just getting to meet Shinozuka-san and all the others was reason enough to be grateful for the chance to chair the committee.

Knowledge, experience, encounters. These would have

been plenty, but heaven sent me one more thing: pressure.

Our biggest worry was money. The corporate support we were counting on was slow in coming, since few businesses would donate to an event like ours during a recession. I went calling on companies with Shinozuka-san, but it was tough.

We also canvassed government offices in search of sponsors. The Ministries of Transport, Health and Welfare, Labor, Construction, Education; the Management and Coordination Agency; the Prime Minister's Office. Quite a whirlwind tour for a mere student, but I couldn't relax enough to enjoy it. I could only tag along after Shinozuka-san, racked with nerves. I sound like a wuss, I know, but as a twenty-one-year-old newbie it was the best I could do.

I might be known for my love of festivals and such, but this symposium wasn't in the same league as a middle school event or a high school movie project. The total budget was close to four million yen (about $40,000 at the time). We were renting the Waseda University International Conference Center, which seats 550. And the fact that we'd be charging participants ¥2,000 (nearly $20), not cheap by any means, was another heavy responsibility.

Travel allows us to dream, adds spice to our lives, brings us closer to nature, lets us meet new people. Most people can enjoy all the travel they have money and time for. But no matter how much time or money they've got, disabled and elderly people don't have the same freedom. As organizers of an effort to look at what prevents people with physical constraints from traveling freely and to find solutions, we had to make the maximum possible impact on society.

Just knowing that I was chairing such an important event felt like a crushing weight on my shoulders.

It's Over . . .

"From Barrier-Free Access to Universal Design 1997" took place on December 14.

The keynote speaker was a writer of popular TV dramas, Toshio Kamata. I was the one who suggested him, even though he doesn't have much connection with welfare services. I didn't want us to be satisfied with just putting on an event even if nothing much changed as a result, in the old way of social service get-togethers. I thought we needed a speaker who could catch the attention of people not already involved and get them to come along. And so we decided to invite Mr. Kamata, who has a lot of appeal for my own generation.

The other highlight of the program was a concert with signing for the hearing-impaired by Shigeki Torizuka, of the sixties pop group the Wild Ones, and his family. The Torizukas are very active giving barrier-free concerts around the country, and have also put out Japan's first signed music video. It was a great concert that brought the whole audience together, signers and nonsigners all "singing along" as one. Some people said afterward it was the most moving thing they'd done in a long while.

This first half of the program really broke the ice, then in the afternoon we divided up for various workshops. Serious debates on transport environments, on systems and policies, on information and services took place as the participants found out about efforts going on in different parts of the country. These forums made their mark; for example, the work of one of the speakers, a Buddhist priest, was subsequently covered in a leading national newspaper.

The long day reached its climax. I rolled out on stage to give the closing speech as chairperson of the organizing committee.

". . . . ."

No words came. This had never happened to me before. When I tried to speak, the lump in my throat wouldn't let me. Instead of giving my prepared speech, I simply said the things that came to mind, lingering over each word, then retreated to the wings. The chairperson had wimped out yet again. Now it was all over.

Maybe the others had started clearing up already, because there was nobody else around the stage area. I let out a huge sigh. Just then I heard a door open and somebody come in. It was Shinozuka-san.

"You've had a long day," he said.

At the sight of his smiling face, all the tension that had built up inside me suddenly gave way. I guess I should have smiled back and said "You too," but instead he got tears for an answer.

"It's over . . . It's over, Shinozuka-san."

"You did a great job. A really great job."

I went on sobbing like a child for the longest time.

The symposium taught me a lot, and in getting to meet everybody involved I was surprised and inspired to learn how many people there are, all over the country, working on these issues in their different ways. At the same time, it seemed to me that much of the energy and enthusiasm was going to waste. I had the feeling that our efforts could be twice as effective if they weren't so fragmented.

Social attitudes are definitely changing. Now is the time to join hands and act. If we scan far and wide to learn what's being done in different places, and share our information, we can change the world. Toward a truly free twenty-first century.

American Travel Notes

San Francisco, City of Hills and Mist

The vacation I took in February 1998 was one I'll never forget. I left home for a three-week trip to the West Coast of the U.S.A. Our group had five members, most of us friends from cram school. Though we'd traveled together in Japan, it was, of course, the first time I'd been overseas. To complicate things, while I'd always used a manual wheelchair for travel in Japan, this time I decided to go with my power chair, though I knew it might be asking for trouble. How the trip would turn out was anybody's guess . . .

First of all, I can't leave out the hassles at San Francisco Airport. When I fly, my power chair has to go as checked baggage. This is tricky. Because the battery is classed as hazardous material, all the cables have to be detached. At Narita Airport our airline took so long over this we thought we'd never get on board, but the real test was after we arrived. Maybe the folks at Narita and SFO got their wires crossed or something, because the ground staff told us they didn't know how to reconnect the cables. Aaarggh! We ended up having to do it ourselves, and by the time we reached Customs we were a wreck.

The moment we got out of the airport, though, we were in a different world. My first impression was the blueness of the sky. We took a ferry ride to see the Golden Gate Bridge, often described as the most beautiful bridge in the world, and the prison that was once home to Al Capone, Alcatraz. It was great—the sky was clear, the breeze felt good, and at the sight of the Stars and Stripes fluttering at the stern, I had the feeling I was really in America.

After two or three days enjoying the scenery, the city, and the stores, we visited Berkeley, which is said to be the most livable community in the States for wheelchair users. I'd heard there were many students in wheelchairs at UC Berkeley, and asked my friends to include it on our program.

"Campus Festa '98" was in full swing that day, and the place was jumping. There were ingenious displays and booths everywhere— it was exciting just to roam around. I was surprised at how many Asian-American students there were among all the black and white faces on campus, but what surprised me most was the number of wheelchairs. I must have seen at least a dozen in the few hours we were there.

Something felt odd, though. I began to notice it while jostling through the crowd. Then it clicked: nobody was paying any attention to me. In Japan, if a guy in a wheelchair makes his way through a crowd, he's always stared at to some degree; here, he wasn't worth a second glance. That told me how ordinary the presence of wheelchairs and disabled people must have become.

In fact, I realized, I'd been noticing all along that my eyes hardly ever met those of passersby, not only in Berkeley but from the moment we'd arrived in America. It was a little dissatisfying for one who likes to be the center of attention, but this, I felt, was the way it should be.

The next day, to celebrate the birthday of a member of our group, we went to see *The Phantom of the Opera*. None of us had ever been to a ritzy theater in Japan, and we were very embarrassed when we got there to find practically everyone else dressed up to the nines. There was a five- or six-year-old boy next to me wearing a tuxedo. And me in a sweater —I must have looked like a real slob.

I was, of course, shown to the wheelchair section. What surprised me, though, was the theater's pricing system. In Japan, no matter how much you've paid or how good a seat you've reserved, you often end up being shown to a wheelchair seat off in a corner and getting into a fight with the usher. This happens not only at the theater but at concerts and sports stadiums too. In America the admission price for wheelchair users is fixed right from the start, which must save a lot of trouble.

There were two or three other people watching the play from the wheelchair section, all looking just as glitzy as the rest of the audience. The lady on my right wore a purple dress with so many spangles it was, like, "Pow!" It was amazing—we disabled people in Japan ought to follow their example and dress with more pizzazz.

Las Vegas, the Desert City That Never Sleeps

After five days in San Francisco, we headed for Las Vegas. If San Francisco is a city of natural beauty, Las Vegas can boast artificial beauty. Every hotel—the whole town, in fact—is a theme park. Next door to a pyramid, there's a medieval European castle; next to that, the Statue of Liberty. Just down the street, pirates are rampaging while beyond them a volcano erupts. And so on. It gets to the point where, watching the most beautiful sunset, you start wondering if that too is being turned on by one of the hotels.

Oddly enough, my wheelchair didn't get along with Las Vegas's luxurious hotels at all. The culprit was their plush wall-to-wall carpeting. My tires sank into the deep pile and got stuck. It reminded me of wheeling along a beach.

The main attraction in Las Vegas is, of course, the casinos. I tried the slot machines with no luck at all. Then, since one of our group was under the legal age for other types of gambling, we all headed for a bingo parlor. Checking the numbers as they flashed onto a huge screen was a real nail-biter. (No nails, did someone say? Picky, picky.) But even if you lose at this high-tension game, it's not that big a disappointment, because it feels like you've gotten your money's worth in entertainment.

The interesting thing was the age of the other players: almost everyone there, besides us, was a senior citizen. This sort of made sense to me. Gambling, which doesn't take much muscle power, is just the thing for older people with time and money to spare. Maybe we'll get casinos in Japan, too, now that the "aged society" is just around the corner.

Within easy reach of Las Vegas there are national parks in every direction, including the Grand Canyon, and we'd booked a rental car to do a tour. It turned out, though, that the agency didn't have a vehicle available with a wheelchair lift. We phoned around but couldn't find one anywhere. I was puzzled how such a thing could happen in America, land of the disabled (?), but I'm told disabled Americans who travel a lot have their own cars equipped with lifts. Okay, I get it . . . I think. In the end, we rented a van big enough to take my chair, removed the back seat, and loaded it in.

Driving around the national parks, we experienced the grandeur—and the harshness—of nature in a way you don't in Japan. Death Valley is said to be the hottest place in the Western Hemisphere, and also the lowest point below sea level. Even in winter, the sun's rays were painfully intense; in summer the temperatures soar above 130°F. At Bryce Canyon, on the other hand, our ears burned in the cold, while the drinks we'd left in the van turned to ice. The clustered spires of rock, carved by wind and water over the ages, are aptly called "nature's sculptures." And I'll never forget the pink flush of sunrise at Lake Powell.

Los Angeles, Largest City on the West Coast

Among all the sights that people associate with Los Angeles —Hollywood, the mansions of Beverly Hills, Santa Monica's beautiful beaches—the one I looked forward to most was Universal Studios. You don't have to be a serious film fan to have a ball at the theme park there, visiting the sets of classic movies that are old favorites in Japan too, and maybe even seeing an actual shoot in progress.

First you take a tram tour through the studio lots, which cover a tremendous area. Then there are so many attractions it's hard to know where to start. Rides to the world of *E.T.* or *Back to the Future*. Heroic stunt displays, infernos raging before your eyes, being attacked by King Kong. All spectacular, but the high point is "The Ride," the Jurassic Park River Adventure. After you've come face-to-face with dinosaurs galore, for the finale, the boat plummets head first down a waterfall.

The wheelchair access was perfect. In Japan, you don't much feel like going to amusement parks when you're in a wheelchair, and if you do, you generally end up just getting tired, but this was a different story. At the live shows there was wheelchair seating right in the front row, and you could board the rides directly from your chair. Accessible toilets were available as a matter of course, and you could search the whole park without finding a single step. In America, even the entertainment industry goes all the way to accommodate people with disabilities. Only in America.

The trip to the States was filled with so many experiences that I can't begin to mention them all here. I wouldn't have missed those three weeks for anything. To say I had a good time is putting it lightly. My parents seemed surprised and impressed, and happy too, that I could go abroad on my own without any assistance from them.

People said it was brave of me, but the courage really belonged to my friends. For college students, a three-week overseas trip must seem a little dicey under any conditions.

But they chose to take a potential troublemaker along with them.

I did cause some hassles due to wheelchair troubles, not to mention my natural-born insistence on having my own way, but it was a wonderful trip. Thanks, fellas. Let's do it again sometime.

On a Snowy Day

You Ever Got Problems, You Give Me a Call

I've been driving a power wheelchair for nearly twenty years now. When you use a wheelchair for as long as that, all sorts of things happen. I'd like to tell you about a few of them here.

This was while I was in cram school. As I've mentioned, the school was in Okubo, Shinjuku Ward. Okubo is a well-known multiethnic neighborhood. When I made my way home at night after working late, the atmosphere in the streets was very different from the daytime. Instead of Japanese, the snatches of conversations I heard were in other Asian languages, which always made the men sound as though they were arguing. And then there were the foreign ladies of the night picking up male passersby in broken Japanese. They seemed to be from many parts of the world, mainly Asia and South America. They would begin to appear at a certain hour after dark, gathering in twos and threes on the streets.

One wintry evening, I'd finished studying and was heading home through drizzling rain. It was too much trouble to use my umbrella, and so I was getting wet as I motored along. But after a while I got so cold I couldn't stand it, and stopped in front of a vending machine that sold cans of hot coffee. I hadn't thought about my next move, though. I can't take money out of my wallet or get a can out of a vending machine by myself. Um. Problems.

Just then, one of the foreign working girls came over to me.

"‡*¥Ø¿*&#Ç."

At least, that's what it sounded like. It didn't seem to be English. I tried saying, in English, that I was very cold and wanted a can of coffee, but, just as I thought, she didn't understand.

She got my meaning, though, when she saw where I was looking and the way I was shivering nonstop. She calmly took out some change from the pocket of her jeans and pointed to the machine as if to ask, "Which kind?" I shook my head, "No, no!" I certainly wasn't expecting her to buy it with her own money when I had mine on me. She watched me with a puzzled look.

But if she didn't understand English, there was no way to get across "Take my wallet out of my pants pocket and buy it for me." I decided I'd just have to let her treat me.

With a rumble and a clank, the eagerly awaited can dropped from the dispenser. She popped the top before handing it over. She was a thoughtful woman who noticed stuff like that. I ought to talk to her about something, I thought, and yet we had no common language. We stayed there together without a word as I drank the coffee. But she was smiling the whole time. A longhaired guy in a wheelchair and a foreign hooker: we must have made quite a pair.

After that, I ran into her several more times on my way home at night. Each time her Japanese had gotten better, and she told me that her name was Milena. One day, she handed me a ten-digit number scribbled on a scrap of paper, then took out her cell phone and kept pointing at it. She seemed to be telling me to call her any time. Not long afterward, though, I noticed she didn't seem to be around any more.

Milena wasn't my only contact with the foreign women of Okubo. One day, an Asian woman called out to me on my way to school. When I stopped and looked back, wondering what she wanted, I saw her rummaging in her bag. Then, believe it or not, she took out several thousand-yen bills and held them out to me. I shook my head, "No, no!" but she stuffed them in my pocket and ran off. It all happened in a flash.

I've heard that quite a few of the foreign women who come to work in the trade in Japan have sick or disabled children back home, and they're here to earn the money for their treatment. That may be why, when they see a disabled person like me, they can't leave him alone.

Another story: One time, I'd arranged to meet a friend at Takadanobaba Station. Standing next to me was a scary-looking character with a *yakuza*'s (gangster's) haircut and dark glasses. I guess he was waiting for someone, too. When five minutes had gone by and my friend still hadn't showed up, he spoke to me.

"Hey, kid."

"Y-y-yes?" My heart sped up—was he going to pick a fight?

"Tough break, huh?"

"Pardon?" This wasn't what I'd expected at all. Suddenly I relaxed.

"Accident?"

When I answered, "I was born like this," he grunted, "Yeah?" in a tone somewhere between shock and sympathy. Then he started telling me about his work.

It was a most interesting subject, and after we'd been deep in conversation for a while I'd completely lost my fear of him. Where *was* my friend, though? He was already fifteen minutes late.

The guy was worried too. "Your pal isn't showing?"

"No, he isn't, is he?"

"He's a lousy friend to keep a good kid like you waiting."

Just in case he was planning to give my friend hell the moment he appeared, I hurriedly made an excuse: "Oh, no, I got here too early."

A while later, he said, "Hey kid, sorry but I gotta go," and reached inside his jacket. My heart skipped a beat, but what he brought out was a business card.

"You ever got problems, you give me a call, okay?" He tucked the card into my pocket and was gone.

Maybe these guys, with their underworld code of honor, like to look out for people like me.

There's a bit more to the story, actually. When I got home I told my parents about the encounter, thinking they'd be surprised, but my mother said coolly, "Well, it stands to reason."

"How come?"

"When those gentlemen have to lop something off, it's never more than their little finger. But you're lopped all over. Of course they're going to respect you."

My father and I just looked at each other.

The Well-Dressed Disabled Man-about-Town

The stereotype that disabled people are to be pitied is still with us, it seems. The foreign women in Okubo and the tough guy in Takadanobaba were probably kind to me because they felt sorry for me. I'm not saying there are *no* pitiful disabled people around: some may have such unpleasant characters that nobody wants to know them. I'd certainly feel sorry for those people, but not because they're disabled. That they're disabled is just a coincidence—it's what's inside that matters.

But I wouldn't say that outward appearances don't count for anything, either. On the trip to the States, I was really struck by the way disabled Americans dress. The natty elderly gent I saw wheeling through downtown San Francisco, the woman sitting next to me at the theater in her sparkly dress. What they had was pizzazz. And it occurred to me to wonder whether people could look at someone like that and think, "Oh, the poor thing."

There are very few snazzy dressers among disabled people in Japan. Maybe it's because they don't get out much in the public eye, but, whatever the reason, the difference is there. For the sake of convenience, perhaps, many Japanese with disabilities stick to something like a parka for everyday wear.

If you take one disabled person who dresses with style and another who always wears the same old parka, even if they both have the same disability and the same kind of lifestyle, it's obvious which one will appear "pitiful" to the rest of the world.

Some folk will no doubt say that what anybody wears is their own business. But I wish that we people with disabilities would take more pleasure in the way we dress, both to change society's image of us, and to give a lift to our own lives.

I've been fussy about clothes ever since I was a kid. I was never satisfied unless I got to wear my favorite gear for a birthday or an outing, and if for some reason my mother couldn't get it washed in time, I pouted and sulked.

At middle school we wore a uniform. Yohga's uniform had a blazer, which didn't offer as much scope for improvement as the typical jacket you'd find at other schools with its naval-style high-buttoned collar. But there was one stylish feature: the necktie. By taking out the cotton stiffener, we could make the knot look skinny and sinister. To adults it may have just looked crummy, but it was the fashion at the time. I took the stiffener out of my tie in imitation of Yatchan, which really annoyed the teachers.

And I'm still a fashion victim today. You can tell how much I love clothes from the fact that when I'm asked what my interests are, since I don't have any true hobbies, I answer, "Going for walks and shopping." My favorite store is Margaret Howell. Although one of her department-store specialty shops is closer to where I live, my all-time favorite is the Margaret Howell store in Jingumae. It carries one-of-a-kind imports, it's spacious and has no steps, so I can browse comfortably in my wheelchair, and the staff are friendly.

There's one snag, however: like the other name designers, Margaret Howell holds sales twice a year, and they happen right at the same time as term tests. No prize for guessing which gets priority with me.

January 15, 1998. It was Coming-of-Age Day, which was of no interest to me because I'd attended the ceremony the previous year; instead, my head was full of the Margaret Howell sale starting that day. But it was snowing out. On the news, they were talking about a record snowfall—practically a blizzard—in the Tokyo area.

It certainly made me hesitate. I was almost on the point of giving up and staying home, but the temptation of those twice-yearly bargains was too much for me. Even my mother was horrified. You have to feel sorry for the mother of a son who's *that* stupid.

A power wheelchair against the snow: it was a really bad idea. The snowdrifts buried my front wheels and stopped me in my tracks. Somehow I made it to the bus stop, with a big sigh of relief. It may have been my imagination, but the driver and passengers seemed to be in shock as they watched me board the bus.

I finally reached the store, half an hour behind schedule, as I'd feared. The sale was under way and the store was packed with customers who'd got in first. One of the sales assistants gasped, "I never thought you'd come in this weather, Ototake-san," as I rushed into the fray.

When I left the store with my trophies—a sweater that would be great for my trip to the States, and a blue shirt that I'd had my eye on—another battle with the snow awaited me. This time, I really got stranded. I had come to a complete standstill (sitstill?) in the bitter cold, when a young man in a business suit passed by.

"What's up? Are you stuck?"

"Yes, I am. The front wheels won't grip, and I can't move at all."

"Okay, wait a sec." Handing me his briefcase and his jacket, he went around in back. Then, taking care not to go for a slide himself, he pushed with all his might.

When he'd pushed me as far as the main street, where the snow was mostly melted, he panted, "Will you be okay here?"

"Yes, that's a great help, thank you very much."

"You must have some *really* important business to be out in a wheelchair in this snow, but you take care, now—don't overdo it."

I wished the pavement would swallow me up.

About My Father and My Mother

My Name, Hirotada

Here, I'd like to introduce you properly to the folks who brought me up, my father and my mother.

My father got married at thirty-three, and I was born when he was thirty-five. So of course that makes him a sensible, dignified father, right? Uh-uh. In many ways, he's more childish than I am.

He sulks when his favorite baseball team, the Yomiuri Giants, is losing. If there's an extra portion of dessert, he always fights me for it. He tries desperately to hum along with pop stars on TV when he doesn't even know the latest hits.

He claims "I'm making sure you don't get spoiled, that's all. Because you're an only child, I have to double as your brother. I'm just being a good father." But it doesn't look to me like he's acting a part.

All the same, this attitude of his is a big plus for our relationship. There's no formality, no sense of his being an authority figure; he really feels more like a friend. We go out together on our days off, and sometimes I meet him at his office after work and we have dinner on the way home. He's a playful, fun kind of dad.

I don't know if it goes with the job—he's an architect—but he cares a lot about style. He designed the house we live in now, and my friends almost always admire it the first time they come over.

He's a style hound himself, not just in his designs. As you'd expect of the man who calls himself "the fashion leader of West Shinjuku," he's fastidious about clothes. It's great for a son, having a father who never stops strutting his stuff. I guess it's pretty much my dad's influence that makes me want to be the type of man who still looks good as he gets older.

It was my father who named me Hirotada (洋匡). He chose the character *hiro* (ocean) to signify "a heart as big as the Pacific Ocean," and *tada* (right) to stand for "setting the world to rights." What's more, *tada* (匡) looks similar to the character for country (国), which consists of a king (王) surrounded by borders, but in the case of *tada* one side is open. The way he sees it, *tada* represents a king who can move about freely and has plenty of get-up-and-go.

My father doesn't usually bother much with finicky details, but in choosing my name he put in quite a bit of work with dictionaries and reference books to find out if various characters would make a lucky combination.* According to

* In the traditional numerology that people in Japan use in choosing names, whether a combination is lucky depends on the number of strokes it takes to write the characters.

his research, the number of strokes in "Hirotada" means that someone with that name will be blessed with the love of many people.

"Setting the world to rights with a heart as big as the Pacific Ocean." I'm not sure whether I've turned out capable of living up to such a grand name, but I've certainly been blessed with the love of many people. I'm proud of my name.

Now's Our Chance! To Hong Kong!

When I was in first and second grade, my mother accompanied me to and from school and waited on standby in the halls all day long.

Takagi Sensei says, "The parents of a disabled child generally tend to make a lot of demands on the school, but Ototake's mother never did that. She entrusted everything to me, which made my job more straightforward."

Although Sensei did consult my mother first before banning the use of my power wheelchair, even then she apparently didn't second-guess his decisions about my education at all. "At school," she told him, "we'll leave everything up to you."

She never interfered unnecessarily where I was concerned, either. When I first started school, Sensei says it made him very nervous to see the other kids coming up to me to ask why I had no arms and legs, or touching my arms with wondering looks; some of them even used to imitate me by tucking their hands and feet up inside their clothes. My mother, however, just said coolly, "It's a problem he has to solve for himself." Sensei remembers being astonished that she could remain so calm while her son was being made a public spectacle like that, but at the same time he sensed a bond of trust between us.

I don't know whether my mother took the attitude she did because we trusted each other, but it's true she almost never interfered in my affairs. Take the summer of seventh grade, for example.

"Uh, this summer, I want to go on a trip to Aomori with a friend . . . " It was the first time I'd suggested anything like this, and I was expecting opposition—I felt sure she'd say, "No, not with just your friend, it's too risky," or maybe, "Will you be all right without us coming along too?" So I was thrown off balance by her reply.

"Oh, that's nice. Be sure to tell us the dates in advance."

"Huh? Okay, sure, but why?"

"Because then, you know, we can go on vacation too."

And when August came, after waving good-bye to me and my friend as we set off for Aomori, my parents caught the next plane to Hong Kong. At this point, you start to sense something here that can't be neatly summed up in terms of "bonds" or "trust." But actually I think this happy-go-lucky attitude of theirs was all for the best.

There's a tendency for the parents of disabled children to be overprotective. Not the Ototakes, though: *they* gaily seize the chance to zip off on vacation while their son's away. Gee, a disabled person just gets no respect around here! But seriously, they had the right approach.

I think one factor that makes a disabled child's parents too protective is a tendency to see him or her as a "poor darling"—with the emphasis on "poor." Children whose parents feel sorry for them will pick up on this feeling very quickly. And they might develop a negative outlook on life: "You have to feel sorry for people with disabilities. Poor me."

A child raised by folks like mine grows up a bit dense, unable to recognize his own disability until he's over twenty, instead of at the usual age of four or five. As a result, I was able to grow up in a free and easy way, without going through a lot of turmoil and self-doubt.

You often hear people talk about "overcoming" or "conquering" a disability, but such expressions don't apply to me and my parents at all. We don't see a disability as an especially negative thing.

It's often said that a disability is "part of a person's individuality." To me, that sounds a little too flattering, and I get the feeling that to nondisabled people it sometimes just sounds like bluffing. As a child, I wrote of my disability as a "strong point," but now I've come to think of it as nothing more than a physical trait. Like fat/thin, tall/short, dark/light. Along with all these variations, there's nothing strange about there being people with/without the use of their limbs. When you think of it like this, there's no reason to brood over a mere physical trait.

It was my parents who taught me to think this way, by example. I am truly grateful to have received life from these two. And thanks, guys, for bringing me up.

Barrier-Free Hearts

Shoes and Wheelchairs

One often sees a notice beside the elevators in Japanese department stores, libraries, and other public places: "Persons in wheelchairs please use only when accompanied." But it's possible for me to do the whole series of actions— steering my power chair into the elevator, pressing the button for the floor I want, and getting off there—on my own. Do I really need someone to accompany me?

Such notices probably reflect a belief that it's dangerous for wheelchair users to be by themselves. Or perhaps the underlying idea is that the disabled are helpless people whom society must look after. But is there any truth in this assumption? A fundamental question which I'd like to look at here.

Sad to say, in Japan today it *is* hard for people with disabilities to move about freely, and it's not easy for us to live on our own. So there's no denying the fact that we need a great deal of help. But it's the environment that forces us into that position.

213

I always think that with the right environment, a person with physical handicaps like mine would not be disabled. When (as is mostly the case in Japan today) there are no elevators in train and subway stations, and I can't board a bus or take a taxi in my wheelchair, it becomes difficult, or even impossible, for me to get from point A to point B. I'm certainly "disabled" then.

But suppose there was an elevator in every station; suppose trains were designed for easy boarding, with no gap or height difference between the edge of the platform and the floor of the car; suppose buses and taxis had lifts for wheelchairs. Then, in using the public transport system (which is all-important in Japanese cities), I would have no disability.

Generally speaking, the Japanese get into their shoes at the door as they leave the house; in my case, I get into a wheelchair instead. That's the only difference. As far as traveling from A to B under our own power is concerned, there's no difference at all.

It's the present environment that makes people "disabled." It also makes others feel sorry for us because of all the things we "can't do" due to physical barriers.

When talking to children, I often say, "Some of you wear glasses, right? Because your vision isn't perfect, right? I use a wheelchair because my legs aren't perfect." They laugh and say, "It's the same thing." However, when I ask if they feel sorry for people who wear glasses, nobody does, yet when I ask, "Do you feel sorry for people in wheelchairs?" just about everybody answers, "Yes."

"But you just told me it's the same as wearing glasses," I say. "Why feel sorry for the person in the wheelchair?" They answer, "A person with bad eyesight can see just fine with glasses, but a person in a wheelchair still can't do a lot of things, so you really have to feel sorry for them."

I think they've hit the nail on the head. What this means is that the conditions that make people with disabilities "pitiful" can be changed—and when it comes to the number of pitiful people, of course, the fewer the better.

A society in which everybody can function freely: it may be a distant ideal, but the day has to come when it will be a reality.

Familiarity Will Do It

How to remove the physical barriers that are so hard on disabled people? I feel that the key is first to remove the "barriers of the heart." After all, we humans create the transport systems, the buildings, the streets and campuses. Depending on how well we understand and work with the needs of disabled people and the elderly, we can make the physical environment that we ourselves build as barrier-free as we want.

Where does that understanding and awareness come from? I think it's worth looking at the part played by familiarity.

Japanese readers may have had the experience of seeing a disabled person in difficulties at a station but not knowing what to say or how to offer help. It's sheer unfamiliarity that makes people hesitate like that and end up walking on by. Afterward, they're often disgusted with themselves, wondering why they didn't speak up. But I don't think they

215

should blame themselves. Even now, you don't come across many disabled people in the streets or on the trains in Japan, and it's not easy to know how to approach people with whom you've had so little contact.

If a foreign family moves in next door, it may take a little while, but we eventually stop thinking of them as "the —s from wherever" and start thinking of them as "our neighbors the —s." With so few opportunities for contact, however, it may be close to impossible for most Japanese to get used to being around disabled people. And so I think that children's experiences hold the key.

Children don't yet have mental barriers in place. When I appear before a school group to give a talk, after an initial flurry of excitement the room becomes very quiet. The kids are goggle-eyed. But after I've spoken for half an hour, they'll start calling me "Oto" while we're having lunch or playing a simple game together, and by the time I'm ready to leave they'll be saying, "Come back and see us again!"

Although they were wary of my weird appearance at first, they've realized I'm an ordinary young man, and they've let their guard down. Kids are very flexible in that way. It's adults who draw a line between "the disabled" and "the able-bodied." In the world of children, anything is possible.

This was true in my own days at kindergarten and primary school. The other kids were up-front with their questions: why, why, why? And as long as I was up-front too and gave them honest answers, they were happy to be my playmates. It was as if whether I had arms and legs or not was all the same to them.

Often a child passing me in the street will go, "Look,

that man has no arms and legs! Why, Mommy?" The flustered mother ducks her head to me in apology, then with a sharp "Never mind, come on!" she drags the child away.

I always think: Ah, what a shame. There goes a chance for one more person to get to know and understand people with disabilities. Children are genuine: when they see a disabled person they want to know "Why?", but once the mystery is solved they treat him like anybody else. I want them to fire away with *more* questions, because it's the questions that aren't asked, and the questions that aren't answered, that form mental barriers. When they're cleared up and kids begin to feel at ease with disabled people, then we begin to see truly "barrier-free" minds and hearts.

My friends often say, "It's true I was shocked the first time I saw you. I didn't know how to behave around you or what to talk about. But after we got talking in class and started going out for a bite to eat together, somewhere along the line I lost track of the fact that you're disabled. So it's only when someone says, 'How about we all take a trip?' that I go, 'Oh, right, you're disabled, aren't you, Oto? So let's think about how you can come along in your wheelchair.' "

I owe my friends for this, of course, but at the same time it's kind of an obvious thing. A particular disability may require special arrangements, but there's no special way of relating to a fellow human being just because he's disabled.

If people feel a higher than necessary barrier the first time they meet a disabled person, it can't be helped. But if time goes by and they still feel some barrier which can no longer be excused by unfamiliarity, personally, I think the disabled person is responsible.

Whether or not an able-bodied and a disabled person get along well together depends on their personalities and whether they're each other's type; it's no different from whether two nondisabled people get along.

And if a guy (or girl) is still hard to be around after you've known him for a while, there's no need to force yourself to be friends out of misguided sympathy. If he goes on about how you're discriminating against him, set him straight: "It's your personality I can't stand!"

Being Ourselves

In order to dissolve our mental barriers, I think that, as well as familiarity, we need a willingness to let others be themselves. I expect the reason that disabled people are said to have easier lives in Western societies is because Westerners are willing to let other people be who they are. Where a great many ethnic groups live in one nation, as in the U.S.A. or parts of Europe, if you rejected others because they were different in the way that happens in Japan, there'd be no end to it. As one minority among many, disabled people in the West tend to be viewed the same way: when seen from the viewpoint of "diversity," a disability is simply accepted as a trait of that person.

The Japanese, however, have always lived as an almost mono-ethnic nation. Sameness is the general rule, and people dread stepping outside its boundaries. Discrimination and prejudice await those who do. In such a society, it may not be easy for people with disabilities to be accepted.

Take the bullying that's a current problem in Japan, especially in junior high schools. The reason kids give is nearly always "He's different from us in this or that way." If they could learn to let others be themselves, most cases of bullying wouldn't happen. Of *course* the other kid is different—everybody is.

And the willingness to accept others begins with knowing your own worth. I started working on the barrier-free campaign because I felt there was something that only I could do. But I'm not the only one who's been given a part to play. All of us have something that only we can do. Some people find it while they're young, some come to it later. Some people probably look back as they approach death and realize, "Ah, *that* was my role in life." In my case, I guess I happened to catch on early because, in having a disability, I had a clear sign. But whether or not we know it yet, we each have our own part to play.

This is only common sense. One can search the world over and not find another person exactly like oneself. If each of us is unique, of course each of us will have a unique role. So we ought to value ourselves more. We ought to take more pride in ourselves.

Japanese children and teenagers today often dwell on what they see as their own imperfections (and they're probably not the only kids who do that). If they could just take pride in themselves as one-of-a-kind, irreplaceable beings, they would surely stop putting themselves down and making their own lives harder. And kids who can accept themselves will naturally be able to accept the next person for who he or she is, too—another being as unique and valuable as they are.

This acceptance would certainly go a long way toward creating a barrier-free society where people with disabilities could live more easily, but that's not the only reason why I want to see it happen. I'd like to see everyone live with a proud awareness of who they are so that they don't waste the life they've been given, but live it to the full.

As for me, I hope to be able to live with pride in myself by contributing in some small way to a world of "barrier-free hearts."

Epilogue

The original title of this book was a phrase that I invented, *Gotai Fumanzoku*. When expectant parents in Japan are asked whether they want a boy or a girl, they often answer, "Either is fine. We'll be happy as long as it's *gotai manzoku*." This common phrase means having the body and limbs (*gotai*) all satisfactorily there (*manzoku*). Every parent has different hopes and dreams when a child is on the way, but "*gotai manzoku*" seems to be the minimum condition that will make parents happy.

Yet I was born *fumanzoku*, the opposite of *manzoku*. Instead of everything being there, nearly everything is missing. That ought to make me a disappointment, a son who has failed to meet even the least of his parents' expectations.

But this assumption is obviously wrong. My parents didn't grieve over their child's disability—it was as if they couldn't have cared less about it. They simply said, "Hard work goes with the territory in bringing up any child." And, most important of all, they can see that I'm enjoying myself every day. Surrounded by friends, zipping around in my wheelchair, I'm not dissatisfied with my life in any way.

I'm told that when prenatal tests reveal a disability, the parents nearly always choose not to have the baby.

In a sense, perhaps this reaction can't be helped. If parents-to-be who've had almost no contact with disabled people are suddenly told, "Your child will be disabled," they probably won't feel brave or confident about bringing it up. Even my mother says, "If I'd had prenatal tests and found out that the baby I was carrying had no arms or legs, to be honest, I can't say for certain whether I would have had you."

All of which makes me want to say loud and clear, "Even with a disability, I'm enjoying every single day." It was to send this message—you don't have to be born perfect to be happy—that I chose the English title *No One's Perfect*. Some people are born able-bodied but go through life in dark despair. And some people, in spite of having no arms and legs, go through life without a care in the world. Disability has got nothing to do with it.

Autumn 1998

Appendix

Proposal to the President of Waseda University
August 30, 1997

We, the Waseda Living Community Campaign, are a group working for an environment-friendly and people-friendly community in the Waseda area. The campaign was created after those involved in organizing the Zero Trash Experiment last year were encouraged to broaden their focus to encompass the future of the community as a whole. It brings together people from every walk of life who love the Waseda area and care about its future, including local residents, store owners, university faculty, members of the business community, government employees, and students.

In recent years, the term "barrier-free" has been coming into general use. Barrier-free access is a key concept in making our community people-friendly, and we believe it is one of the most important issues to be addressed.

Looking at Waseda University from this perspective, the reality one sees is that not enough consideration has been given to the needs of people with disabilities. On the historic main campus, certain buildings are difficult even to enter in a wheelchair. For students with limited mobility who cannot leave their wheelchairs, such buildings are nothing but barriers.

As you have said, Waseda University has the fine ideal of being "an open university." But shouldn't a truly open university provide an environment in which students with disabilities have free access to learning?

It will, of course, take time and money to remove existing barriers; there are also likely to be a number of technical issues. Accordingly, we invite you to join with us in studying barrier-free accessibility, including the problems involved in its implementation.

If Waseda University becomes truly open to people with disabilities, it will surely set an example to other universities and greatly encourage the trend to barrier-free access throughout society. It will also be a source of great pride to residents of the district like ourselves. Above all, we believe that Waseda's founder, Shigenobu Okuma, who was maimed by a terrorist bomb [in 1889], would surely want the university he established to be barrier-free. We ask you to consider this proposal favorably so that the university and local residents may come together to build a Waseda community for the twenty-first century.

（普及版）英文版 五体不満足
No One's Perfect / TP

2003 年 12 月　第 1 刷発行
2006 年 6 月　第 2 刷発行

著　者　乙武洋匡
訳　者　ジェリー・ハーコート
発行者　富田 充
発行所　講談社インターナショナル株式会社
　　　　〒 112-8652 東京都文京区音羽 1-17-14
　　　　電話　03-3944-6493（編集部）
　　　　　　　03-3944-6492（マーケティング部・業務部）
　　　　ホームページ　www.kodansha-intl.com

印刷・製本所　大日本印刷株式会社